ROMAN GARDENS

GARDENS

Villas of the City

PHOTOGRAPHS BY ROBERTO SCHEZEN

•

TEXT BY MARCELLO FAGIOLO

THE MONACELLI PRESS

First published in the United States of America in 2001 by
The Monacelli Press, Inc.
10 East 92nd Street, New York, New York 10128.

Library of Congress Cataloging-in-Publication Data
Fagiolo, Marcello, 1941– .
Roman gardens / photographs by Roberto Schezen ; text by Marcello
Fagiolo.
p. cm.
Contents: [1] Villas of the Countryside. [2] Villas of the City.
Includes bibliographical references.
ISBN 1-885254-57-1 (v. 1)   ISBN 1-58093-037-9 (v. 2)
1. Palaces—Italy—Lazio. 2. Architecture, Renaissance—Italy—Lazio.
3. Architecture, Baroque—Italy—Lazio. 4. Gardens, Renaissance—Italy—
Lazio. 5. Gardens, Baroque—Italy—Lazio. 6. Sculpture gardens—Italy—
Lazio. 7. Gardens, Italian—Italy—Lazio. 8. Garden ornaments and
furniture—Italy—Lazio. I. Schezen, Roberto. II. Title.
NA7755.F27   1997
728.8'2'094562—dc21   97-18503

Printed and bound in Italy

Typography by Paul Montie/Fahrenheit
Translated from the Italian by David Stanton

CONTENTS

ROMAN GARDENS

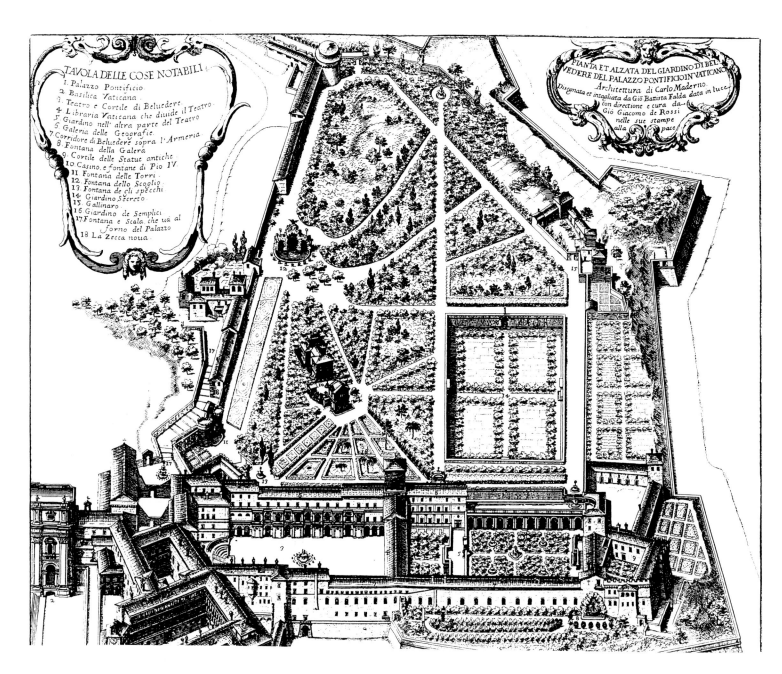

1. View of the Vatican palazzi and gardens (engraving by G. B. Falda, 1676). In the foreground is the Belvedere Court on three levels: the first (3) with the theater built by Pirro Ligorio, the second beyond the Sistine Library (4), and the third (5) with the garden of Julius III. On the right is the villa of Innocent VIII with its octagonal sculpture court (9); below is the Fontana della Galera (8). Beyond this is the boundary wall with fountains dating from the pontificate of Paul V: Fontana delle Torri (11); Fontana dello Scoglio (12); and the Casino of Pius IV (10). Below are the radially planned herb garden dating from Pius V's pontificate (16) and Paul III's walled garden (14).

The villas of modern Rome are linked through cultural ideology to those of imperial Rome; both share a vision of the rebirth of antiquity.[1] In imperial Rome, next to the city of marble (which had replaced the city of mud and wood and the one of bricks) lay the city of gardens, equivalent in size to the built-up area. Between the Servian walls and the Aurelian ones, especially in the area between the Pincian, Quirinal, and Esquiline hills, there was a continuous greenbelt of suburban villas: it was formed by the gardens of Lucullus (*horti Luculliani*) on the Pincian; of Sallust (*horti Sallustiani*) between the Pincian and the Quirinal; and of Lamia (*horti Lamiani*), Maia (*horti Maiani*) and Maecenas (*horti Maecenatiani*) on the Esquiline. The suburban villa, as La Rocca writes,

> *on the one hand offered its owner a place where free time could be spent in leisure and contemplation; on the other it was a very prestigious residence, worthy of a prince. And the ostentatious magnificence was taken to almost a sacred plane, with the gardens and groves surrounding the house becoming, symbolically, the dwelling-place of the gods.*[2]

The *horti*, constructed in areas where land cost much less than in the city center, allowed the aristocracy to live in luxury—forbidden by law since the Republican period—and promote their public images. As Vitruvius explained,

> *For the nobles who are appointed as important magistrates, regal vestibules and vast atria and peristyles must be built, with woods and walks to add luster to their names. In addition, there should be libraries, picture galleries, and basilicas rivaling public buildings in their magnificence.*[3]

Over a thousand years later, in the age of humanism, the architectural type of the villa *all'antica* was revived, modeled on the villas of imperial Rome and the literary accounts of Varro and Pliny the Younger. Bramante, Raphael, Giacomo da Vignola, and their successors reconstructed the settings of the ancient gardens, the suburban villas of the patricians and emperor. The spirit of Nero's Domus Aurea (golden house; fig. 2) and the imperial gardens informed such villas of popes and cardinals as the Belvedere, the villas Madama, Giulia, and Farnese, and the Farnese Gardens. In the case of Pirro Ligorio (ca. 1510–83), the architect who designed the Casino of Pius IV in the Vatican gardens and the Villa d'Este at Tivoli, the emulation of antiquity led to the creation of remarkable gardens of stone in which there is all the theatricality—and even a miniature reconstruction—of ancient Rome.

The villas built on the heights of Rome lend a new significance to those hills, occupied by gardens since ancient times: the Vatican (fig. 1), Janiculum, Esquiline, and Pincian. Next to the Pincian—described as the *Collis hortulorum*—emerged new "hills of gardens," such as the Quirinal, which gradually replaced the Vatican after the Middle Ages. The seventeenth- and eighteenth-century peregrinations of the Arcadian Academy over the various hills of Rome in search of premises are particularly revealing. First it was located on the Janiculum (in the church of San Pietro in Montorio) and then on the Palatine (in the Farnese

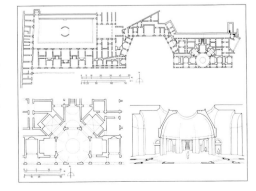

THE VILLAS AND GARDENS OF ROME

2. Plan of the residential area of Nero's Domus Aurea (from H. Stierlin, 1984). At the bottom is the octagonal hall of the *cenatio*, originally covered by the rotating cosmological roof.

Gardens, believed to be the site where Arcadians gave shelter to Aeneas), on the Aventine, and elsewhere before finally establishing itself in the Bosco Parrasio, back on the Janiculum.

In the baroque age, both within and without the city walls and especially in the Tuscolana area, new types of villas were built that served as models for the rest of Europe, although some were destroyed in the nineteenth and twentieth centuries. After the middle of the eighteenth century, in the wake of the vogue for archaeology started by Piranesi and Winckelmann, neoclassical, romantic, and eclectic gardens became popular. The Villa Albani and then, in their turn, the Villa Borghese and the Villa Torlonia became reinterpretations of Hadrian's Villa at Tivoli, reproducing various Mediterranean marvels in a sort of panorama of history.

The Palatine and the Domus Aurea

Before becoming emperor bearing the honorific Augustus, Octavian intentionally acquired his residence on the Palatine—the site of the legendary foundation of Rome—near the "House of Romulus." He then enlarged this house, but without great luxury; a larger palace, the Domus Tiberiana, was built by his successor, Tiberius.

Later Nero planned a wing (Domus Transitoria— a passage, in other words) linking the Palatine with the Esquiline, where the gardens of Maecenas were situated. The terrible fire that destroyed a large part of the palace and two thirds of the city in 64 CE gave the emperor the opportunity both to reconstruct his residence on the Palatine and to build a huge new palace, the Domus Aurea. Seutonius describes the building vividly:

> To give an idea of its extent and splendor, the following will suffice: it had a vestibule in which a colossal statue of Nero was erected, 120 feet in height; it was surrounded by a colonnade with three tiers of columns, a thousand paces in length; and there was also a lake, similar to a sea, overlooked by buildings that formed many cities; beside all this there was a stretch of countryside with cultivated fields,

> vineyards, meadows, and forests, inhabited by all kinds of domestic and wild animals.[4]

Tacitus, astonished by the creation of this landscape or "artificial nature," added,

> It is not so much the precious stones and gold that cause amazement, but rather the cultivated fields, the lakes, and, as in solitary places, on the one hand, woods and, on the other, esplanades with splendid vistas, designed and constructed by Severus and Celer, whose daring creativity allowed art to achieve what nature had forbidden.[5]

The Romans feared that this vast villa or urban park, covering perhaps forty or fifty hectares (100 to 125 acres), would expand until it occupied the whole of the city and its surroundings, as a satirical epigram quoted by Seutonius stated:

> Rome will become Nero's Domus. Romans, migrate to Veii if the Domus does not also incorporate Veii.[6]

The whole city served to promote the public image of the emperor, who considered renaming it Neropolis, while the month of April (associated with the day Rome was founded) would be called neronianius. In another fit of megalomania, Nero initiated huge engineering projects, the only objective of which was his own amusement, involving parts of Latium and Campania. Nero's new design for an "artificial landscape" extended from Rome to Ostia and Campania, in some places superimposing imperial order on the disorder of the marshy areas. In Seutonius's words,

> He started the construction of a piscina that extended from Misenum to Lake Avernus, entirely covered and surrounded by porticos, into which the thermal waters of Baiae were to be fed; then he set about building a canal 160 miles in length from Lake Avernus to Ostia, which was intended to allow boats to arrive there without sailing on the sea.[7]

With the colossal statue of the emperor—who was certainly portrayed as the sun king—standing in the entrance, and the building's orientation—like a *templum caeleste*—aligning exactly with the four cardinal points, the Domus Aurea must have been conceived as a "sun palace" modeled on the residences of the Hellenistic sovereigns or possibly the sun palace described by Ovid.

The architects of the palace, Severus and Celer, were described by Tacitus as *magistri et machinatores* (masters and engineers). They conceived of various technological marvels (described in Seutonius's) account and combined them with a display of wealth that was vaguely oriental in character and unusual in Rome. In his palace, Nero regarded himself as the heir of the oriental kings of kings who styled themselves "kings of the universe" or "kings of the four quarters of the world." In the building, Seutonius writes,

> *everything was covered in gold, precious stones, shells, and pearls; the ceilings of the dining rooms were made of tablets of ivory and crossed by tubes from which flowers and perfumes were scattered over the guests. The most important of these rooms was circular and revolved continuously, night and day, like the world; both seawater and the waters of Albula flowed into the baths. When the palace had been completed and Nero inaugurated it, he limited himself to saying that finally he had a residence worthy of a man.*[8]

In later ages, scholars focused their attention mainly on the round, or rather octagonal, room, which consisted of a dome with an oculus in the center (similar to the later dome of the Pantheon completed in Hadrian's reign). From the room there was a view of a *nymphaeum* with waterfalls. This room may have served as a *cenatio* or *triclinium* (dining room), or as a throne room, and it was evidently covered with a revolving wooden roof resembling the heavens. H. P. l'Orange hypothesized that it was a throne room with a cosmic dome of the type later described in connection with the Persian king Khosroes II.[9] Nero is thought to have personified Helios-Cosmocrator (the sun god and Lord of the World), the motor of the celestial spheres at the center of the universe. The color gold, which covered all the rooms in the palace,

may be linked to the symbolism of the sun. Moreover, during the visit of the Armenian king Tiridates, the emperor played the role of Mithras-Sun during a festival in Pompey's theater, where the walls of the theater were wholly covered in gold and actors wore gilded costumes. The poet Lucan exhorted the emperor to place his throne in the center of the universe:

> *Keep the equilibrium of the firmament in the middle of the sphere of the universe!*[10]

It has also been suggested that there is a reminiscence of the Palace of Atlantis described in Plato's *Critias*. The resemblance is found not only in the large park with piscinas, aqueducts, and an artificial lake for *naumachiae* (mock naval battles staged for entertainment), but also in the central temple surrounded by golden walls and covered with gold and ivory.

Nero's later *damnatio memoriae*—part of the penalty for *maiestas* (treason)—led to the demolition of the Domus Aurea. The Baths of Trajan were built over the remains of the palace; the colossal statue was transformed into a statue of the sun god; and the Flavian amphitheater (later called the "Colosseum" after the huge statue) was constructed on the site of the artificial lake.

It was Domitian who, with great solemnity, brought the imperial residence back to the Palatine (the imperial palace par excellence was named for the Palatine Hill, in Latin *Palatium*). The architect Rabirius designed two hilltop complexes, the Domus Flavia (Flavian house) and the Domus Augustana (house of the emperors), flanked by the "stadium" or "circus," which in reality was probably a garden in accordance with a type described later in Pliny the Younger's letters. Thus a model of the imperial residence or *Palatium*, with stadia and "Palatine" temples, was created; it was reproduced on various occasions throughout antiquity (for instance, in Constantinople, the "second Rome"), in the Middle Ages (the complex of San Marco in Venice), and during the Renaissance (the Vatican Palace with the "Palatine" basilica and the Belvedere Court). Other ancient Roman precedents include the Circus Gai et Neronis (Caligula and Nero's circus) in the gardens of the Vatican, as well as such other later examples as the imperial villa at Porta Maggiore (with the Amphitheatrum Castrense, subsequently incorporated into the Aurelian walls), the Palatium of Maxentius on the Via Appia (with the Circus of Maxentius), the gardens of Sallust (the hippodrome of Aurelian), the villa of the Sette Bassi on the Via Tusculanum (a hippodrome-cum-garden), and the Villa Quinctilii on the Via Appia (two hippodromes).

The Apogee and Decline of the Gardens on the Hills of Rome

Before they were embraced by the Aurelian walls, the gardens allowed a certain degree of control over the access roads and made use of the abundant water supplies provided by the aqueducts. After the fire of 64 CE, Nero incorporated all these gardens into the Domus Aurea. But Tiberius had already included the gardens of Sallust in the imperial estates; after being extended on a number of occasions, they became the most grandiose in Rome and the favorite residence of many emperors. Vespasian held many audiences and receptions there after eliminating the Domus Aurea, and Aurelian practiced riding in the hippodrome—the Porticus Miliarensis—he had built himself. The emperors often stayed in these gardens both for the beauty and amenity of the site and for the proximity of the Castrum Praetorium, the citadel of the imperial army.

The gardens of Sallust seem to have contained many of the elements later reproduced or echoed in modern Rome. Their position between the Pincian and the Quirinal hills appears to be symbolic, with the presence of a circus or hippodrome on the Pincian (perhaps on the site where the obelisk of Sallust was found; it was later erected at Trinità dei Monti) and with the remodeling of the valley in the supposed Forum Sallustii. The position of the *horti inter duos montes* (gardens between two hills) called for large engineering works with substructures, arched retaining walls, and buttresses to create gardens and terracing. Conceived as an intermediary complex between the villa and the Palatium, the gardens of Sallust comprised *nymphaea*, baths, cisterns, and small temples such as the Temple of Venus of Eryx. The most impressive remains, in Piazza Sallustiana, are perhaps those of a dining room dating from Hadrian's reign, similar to the *serapeum* at Hadrian's Villa.

In modern times, the Palazzo del Quirinale and its gardens took over the function of second palace or suburban alternative to the Palatium, while in the first half of the seventeenth century the process of putting archaeological finds from the ancient gardens on display was begun at the Villa Pinciana Ludovisia.

The destruction of the aqueducts at the time of the siege by the king of the Ostrogoths, Vitige, in 537 CE, rapidly depopulated Rome, especially on the hilltops, left without water, while the surviving gardens disappeared completely. It has been estimated that, at the end of the sixth century CE, Rome's population fell below 100,000, with the inhabitants concentrated along the banks of the Tiber. From that time onward the city was no longer divided into built-up areas and gardens, but rather into built-up areas and abandoned ones.

The Vatican as a Villa All'antica

Of paramount importance for the rebirth of the garden *all'antica* was the development of the Vatican gardens, particularly the sixteenth-century projects.[11] We know that during the pontificate of Julius II (1503–13), the plans of Nicholas III (pope 1277–80) and Nicholas V (pope 1447–55) were completed with the construction of a palace "in the form of a city." The studies of Ackerman and Bruschi have thrown light on the real significance of the Belvedere Court,[12] started by Bramante even before the rebuilding of St. Peter's as an example of a palace that was both modern and antique. (According to Vasari, the architect had also planned the total reconstruction of the Vatican Palace.) The court has been described as the first open-air theater after antiquity, the first museum, and the first attempt to integrate a garden and architecture.

3. Plan of the Casino of Pius IV in the Vatican (from Letarouilly, 1857).

The corridor or walkway linking the Vatican Palace and the villa of Innocent VIII (extended with a museum for classical antiquities in the courtyard and perhaps intended to serve as an artists' studio) was transformed into an imposing composition that had parallels only in imperial Rome. Thus, to the north of the Vatican, a space was created that alluded to both the concept of the Palatine stadium or circus and the preexistence of the Circus Gai et Neronis on this site.

The theme of the "circus" was also present in the archaeological and literary tradition of the villa of antiquity. For example, the Tuscan villa of Pliny the Younger and its garden-cum-hippodrome served as a constant source of inspiration for the design of sixteenth-century villas, from Raphael's project for the Villa Madama to the "amphitheater" of the Boboli Gardens. In its turn, the Belvedere Court, with its intermediate levels arranged into garden terraces with staircases, was a model for villas and city planning at least until the baroque period.

4. Casino of Pius IV in the Vatican Gardens (engraving by G. B. Falda, 1676). In the foreground is the sixteenth-century herb garden; the "boschetto del belvedere" and the Fontana delle Torri are visible behind the casino.

The western "corridor" of the Belvedere Court starts at the loggias of San Damaso and ends at the villa and spiral staircase of the Belvedere. In the satirical dialogue *Simia*, composed in 1516 by Andrea Guarna da Salerno, Bramante ascends the steep slopes of the lofty mountain of Paradise, modeled perhaps on the old Vatican's "magnificent walls, soaring towers, and incomparable palaces." When, at the gates of heaven, St. Peter reproaches him for the demolition of the old basilica, Bramante responds with a project for the overall renovation of Paradise, evidently drawing on his proposals for the Vatican:

> I want to remove this road leading from earth to heaven that is so steep and difficult to climb: I shall build another, spiral one that will be so wide that the souls can come up on horseback. Then I think I'll knock down this Paradise and make a new one that will have more elegant and comfortable dwellings for the blessed.

And, on seeing the perplexity of the Prince of the Apostles, the terrible "Maestro Ruinante" even threatens to descend into hell and entirely rebuild it.

Unfinished when Julius II died, the Belvedere Court was completed in various stages over the centuries. The most outstanding contribution, made during the pontificate of Pius IV (1559–65), was that of Pirro Ligorio; it marked the apogee of the court as a multifunctional building. A curved theater was built below the walls of the palace; this was the first construction in stone of a theater *all'antica*. On the opposite side, Bramante's exedra was transformed into a gigantic niche that was both sacred and profane, with a semicircular loggia. Derived from the sanctuary of the Fortuna Primigenia at Palestrina, it foreshadowed Bernini's colonnade in the Piazza of St. Peter's.

The concept of Paradise, found for the first time in Nicholas V's plans for the Vatican, was most clearly expressed in the exquisite little Casino of Pius IV[13] (figs. 3, 4). This remarkable complex of buildings—the actual casino (summer house), the loggia, and two *tempietti*—is built around an oval courtyard that not only pays homage to the Vatican archetype of the *naumachia* (or the lake of the Domus Aurea, reconstructed by the Renaissance antiquaries in an oval form), but is also an image of the city or the citadel (for instance, the reconstructions of ancient Rome and the Capitoline Hill, and the oval of the Piazza del Campidoglio), a symbol of the passing of time and the cycle of the seasons, a "theater of memory," and the visual representation of an all-encompassing, encyclopedic culture.

Like the villa of Innocent VIII, the casino is both an academy and a museum: it is a temple and sanctuary of the Muses on the Vatican Hill transformed into Parnassus. Already Sixtus IV, founder of the Palatine Library, had been termed *Pastor Apollo*; Julius II bore the titles *Alter Apollo* or *Apollo Magus*; and Leo X had been celebrated as Apollo reigning over the Parnassus-Vatican. Now Pius IV, a Medici from Milan, drew upon the ideology of the previous Medici pope, posing as *Apollo Medicus*, or rather *Sol Pacifer*, promoter of a new golden age, the return to earth of Astraea, and the dawn of a renewed world. This is conveyed by the bas-reliefs representing the sun, Aurora-Astraea, and Zeus being suckled by the she-goat Amalthea. Elevated at the center of the "sacred grove" of the Vatican, the casino's other bas-reliefs convey the ancient concept of Parnassus: Apollo and the Muses are portrayed on the loggia, and in the center of the facade, in an aedicule, appears the fabled Mount Pierus in Thessaly, where Zeus coupled with Mnemosyne and the Muses were conceived. "Pierius" (as the name is written in the inscription) is an ambiguous effeminate figure, who may perhaps be identified with memory—Mnemosyne, in other words. The importance given to this mountain (a more likely choice would have been Parnassus or the Helicon instead of the father of the Pierians or "false Muses") is perhaps linked to its *nomen-omen* (its name as a presage): "Pierius" is the humanistic transcription of the name Peter and alludes to the Vatican as a *Mons Pius* (Pious Mountain) in a tribute to the pope (and also, perhaps, a reference to the name of the architect, Pirro, in Latin *Pyrrhus*).

5. Villa Madama (engraving by G. Vasi, 1761). Below the loggia designed by Raphael is the fishpond with a substructure supporting the hanging garden.

From the *Villa Madama* and the *Villa Giulia* to the *Farnese Gardens*

There is a clear link between the Villa Madama (fig. 5), built for the Medici by Raphael,[14] and the Villa Giulia, built for Julius III (pope 1550–55) by a team of architects consisting of Giacomo da Vignola, Giorgio Vasari, and Bartolomeo Ammannati, probably under the direction of Michelangelo.[15] Both villas were built around a series of courtyards placed longitudinally, and the semicircular courtyard of the Villa Giulia was derived from the circular courtyard of the Villa Madama (only half of which was built). Both villas were commissioned by a Tuscan pope, and both lie to the north of Rome, in the direction of Tuscany.

Like the Villa Madama, the Villa Giulia (figs. 6, 7) must have been used for sumptuous receptions; indeed, the two villas were probably intended to be outposts where illustrious guests were received before their solemn—or triumphal—entry into Rome. And,

like the Villa Madama but on a reduced scale, the greatest prominence was given to the balcony from which the pope could command an excellent view of the surrounding area. The unbuilt balcony of the Villa Madama (reconstructed by Frommel as a sacred niche placed above a rustic portal in a manner that was comparable to the Villa Giulia) was to have dominated in one direction, the Via Cassia, or Via Francigena—the main route from Medicean Tuscany toward the Vatican—and, in the other, the loop of the Tiber toward the Ponte Milvio, associated with the crucial victory of Constantine in 312 CE. Raphael, Villa Madama's architect, chose to commemorate the event in the fresco *The Battle at the Milvian Bridge* in the Sala di Constantino in the Vatican, a chamber for lavish receptions. It is no coincidence, therefore, that the villa appears in the background of this painting, added by Giulio Romano (who actually executed the fresco and continued the work on the villa after Raphael's death).

Thus, on one side, the Villa Madama faced outward from the city, toward places of paramount importance for both pagan and Christian Rome: Tuscany, the land of the Etruscans, and the bridge forming a metaphorical link between antiquity and the Middle Ages. (The issuing of Constantine's Edict of Milan, establishing tolerance for Christians, in the year following the battle is considered by many the start of a new era.) On the other side, the villa faced not so much the Vatican as the center of imperial Rome. In fact, if its main axis is extended toward the city, it meets the Colosseum, in the valley surrounded by the famous hills of Rome and associated with Nero's Domus Aurea and the legendary persecution of the first Christians. It is also significant that the balcony of the Villa Giulia—aligned with the semicircular exedra that was clearly derived from Raphael's building—faces in the direction of the Villa Madama; on the other side of the Tiber, it is about 2,300 meters away.

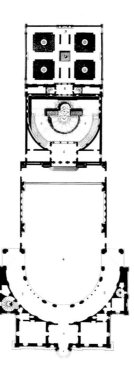

7. The semicircular portico at Villa Giulia, decorated with fictive pergolas (engraving from Percier and Fontaine, 1824).

Intended to be a place for watching and being watched, the Villa Giulia is a concatenation of theaters and spectacles. First, there is the proscenium formed by the point where the Via Iulia Nova (now Via di Villa Giulia) meets the Via Flaminia, with the undulating "wings" of water of the *nymphaea*. Next, the semicircular area at the front of the villa may have been used for open-air entertainments watched by the pope from the balcony. The third "theater" is the large courtyard of the villa. Ammannati wrote:

The avenue is the proscenium, the courtyard the orchestra, the semicircle of the palace is a theater, and what I am about to describe forms the stage-set.

If, therefore, Vignola's hemicycle is the "theater," Ammannati's architecture of the "stage-set" at the end of the courtyard is conceived both as a triumphal arch and *scenae frons* (scene front). From this point of view, the facade presages Palladio's reconstruction of Vitruvius's stage-set, first graphically in Daniele Barbaro's 1556 Italian edition of Vitruvius's *De architectura* and then spatially in the Teatro Olimpico in Vicenza. The architectural structure framing the mythological and allegorical panels may have derived from a famous ephemeral example of "triumphal theater": the wooden theater constructed on the Capitoline Hill in 1513, endowed with the most "decoration, grace, and proportion" since the age of imperial Rome.[16] Indeed, this was considered to be a model for the revival of the antique style and one of the prototypes of the facades *all'antica* of the cinquecento and seicento in Rome, including the Casino of Pius IV in the Vatican, the Villa Medici on the Pincian, and the Villa Doria Pamphili.

The main axis of the Villa Giulia creates a telescoping perspective effect; it is a "permeable axis" along which the openings of portals, arcades, and Serlian motifs are aligned, allowing the observer to see

6. Plan of Villa Giulia (from Percier and Fontaine, 1824). From bottom to top are the villa with the semicircular portico (1–3), the first courtyard (4), the scenic loggia (5), the second courtyard with Ammannati's *nymphaeum* (6, 7), the Serlian loggia (8), and the third courtyard with the Serlian motif forming a backdrop (9).

beyond, courtyard after courtyard, as far as the distant boundary wall. In a spectacular enfilade, through the portal of the villa it is possible to see the "proscenium" of the first courtyard and the Serlian motif of the second one, right up to the bas-relief Serlian motif on the boundary wall, forming a perspective backdrop to the whole composition. It cannot be ruled out that it was Michelangelo who had the initial idea for this scheme, given the "permeable axis" of the Palazzo Farnese, with its view from the piazza as far away as the Tiber through the opening in the end wall of the courtyard and beyond to the palace gardens and the vineyard in Trastevere.

The Farnese Gardens (*Horti Farnesiani;* figs. 8, 9) on the Palatine constitutes one of the most secret visions of a real and imaginary revival of the ancient world. The gardens were designed in three successive stages, linked to the projects of Vignola (1565–73), Jacopo del Duca (1573–77), and Girolamo Rainaldi.[17] The sixteenth-century complex of gardens was conceived as a *cittadella dell'otium* (citadel of leisure), an enclosure reserved for the lord and his guests in the center of his vast estates. Significantly, the portal in ashlar stonework resembles the gate of a fortress, modeled on the Belvedere and the Villa Madama, the two basic prototypes of the villa-fortress. (In particular, the Villa Madama was to have been completed with high, possibly crenelated walls and turrets deriving from the Palazzo Ducale—"a palace in the form of a city"—in Urbino.)

In the Farnese Gardens, the boundary wall—demolished a century ago during the excavations on the Palatine—was characterized by the high scarp crowned by a torus (typical elements of fortifications) and turrets at the ends, possibly used as lookout posts. Perhaps only the boundary wall was built by Vignola, or was at least conceived by him, while the upper part of the portal and the windowed boundary wall were designed by Jacopo del Duca. It is possible, however, that Vignola himself planned the new layout for the slopes of the Palatine; moreover, it should not be forgotten that the early stage of the appropriation of the

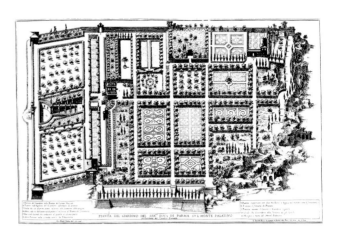

8. Farnese Gardens on the Palatine (engraving by G. B. Falda, 1676).

9. Farnese Gardens on the Palatine (engraving by G. Vasi, 1761). The system of terracing and the flight of steps leading to the seventeenth-century facade of the aviary are evident.

hill took place during the pontificate of the greatest of the Farnese, Paul III.[18] And what was the Palatine like at that time? Apparently, it was nothing more than "a labyrinth of ancient ruins and imposing arches with the remains of stuccoes and frescoes, known as the 'Palazzo Maggiore.'" In 1553 Lucio Fauno wrote:

The Palatine Hill has now returned to its ancient state, since, just as it was previously the place where animals grazed, so some would have liked to call it the "Baalantine" because of the bleating of the sheep, today there are ruins and uncultivated, wild places. . . . But it was always the abode of kings and emperors, as the ruins themselves very clearly demonstrate to the great astonishment of whoever sees them.[19]

Vignola's wall around the gardens forms a square green citadel, a bastion of contemplation on the site of the "square Rome" founded by Romulus on the Palatine. Significantly, the portal is aligned precisely with the basilica of Maxentius, then identified as the "Templum Pacis." The Palatium of the emperors was thus reborn as a garden of stone: in the various stages of construction, the slopes of the hill were laid out in terraces, flights of steps, *nymphaea*, and, ultimately, the twin aviaries that refer to the founding myth of Romulus and Remus sighting the augural birds.[20] In the garden proper, the order of the geometric garden coexisted with the freedom of the Arcadian landscape (it was not by chance that the Arcadian Academy had their premises here for some time), incorporating the romantic ruins of the "Palace of the Caesars."

After the birth of Napoleon's heir—the "King of Rome"—in 1811, the director of the Louvre, Dominique Vivant Denon, suggested that the emperor should create a magnificent garden comprising the Capitoline Hill, the Roman Forum, and the Farnese Gardens, in order to lay out

> *in the center of Rome the most splendid garden in the universe. . . . This beautiful place, planted with trees and irrigated with the abundant waters of the Palatine, would be sown with sublime memories and include the finest monuments of ancient Rome.*[21]

After a lengthy debate, the definitive project by J. M. Berthault was approved in 1813. His design proposed that the whole hill be laid out as a garden; it would be dominated in the center by a large cruciform square oriented toward the "Templum Pacis." This wholesale renewal of the gardens would have resulted in the concealment or sacrifice of some of the remains of the "Palace of the Caesars," in sharp contrast with other French projects that provided for the excavation and conservation of antiquities. Obviously, due to Napoleon's demise, the project was never realized. Seventy years later, a large part of the garden was destroyed to allow for new excavations on the Palatine.

The Revival of the Collis Hortulorum: From the Villa Medici to the Villa Ludovisi

In the fifteenth and sixteenth centuries the Pincian Hill—for which the humanists revived the designation *Collis Hortulorum*—became the hill of contemplation on which the vineyards and estates of the religious orders were located. In the creation of the Villa Medici (fig. 10) by Cardinal Ferdinando de' Medici (later grand duke of Tuscany), the Collis Hortulorum became a model for the design of the villa.[22]

In particular, Ammannati's project (documented in two of Jacopo Zucchi's frescoes in the villa's *studiolo*) clearly indicates the desire to compete with the spectacular layout of the gardens of Lucullus, reconstructed in a famous drawing by Pirro Ligorio. An axial composition clearly influenced by the sanctuary of the Fortuna Primigenia at Palestrina, it comprises the following elements: a rectilinear flight of steps ascending from the level of the Campus Martius to a complex system of double flights of covered transverse steps (recalling both Palestrina and the so-called Temple of the Sun on the Quirinal); a system of double transverse ramps (modeled on the Belvedere Court); an upper square delimited by the celebrated large exedra; and, lastly, a circular temple, described by Ligorio as the "Temple of Three Fortunes—the established, the felicitous, and the propitious." (This identification recalls, on the one hand, the sanctuary at Palestrina and, on the other, through triadic symbolism, the church of Trinità dei Monti.) The temple, described by other authors as "Templum Solis" or "Domus Pincii," appears cylindrical with a roof resembling those of the Pantheon and the temple of Minerva Medica. Partially destroyed during the sixteenth century, it was eventually incorporated into the belvedere mound of the Villa Medici. Ligorio's studies depicting the terraced gardens as a monumental front to the Collis Hortulorum may also be seen as a model for contemporary proposals for the layout of the Pincian Hill's slopes, from Ammannati's project to the various

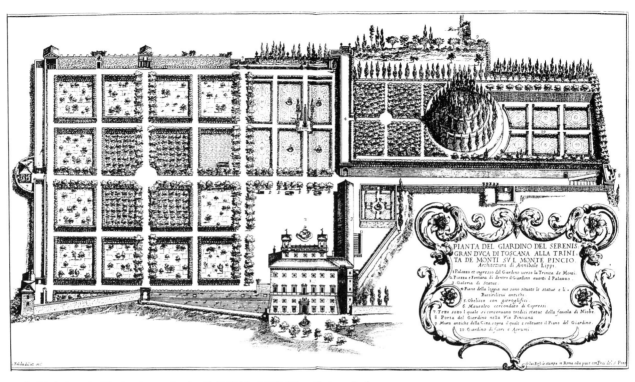

10. Villa Medici on the Pincian (engraving by G. B. Falda, 1676). The villa is at the bottom, the Aurelian walls at the top, and the mound of Parnassus toward the right.

proposals for steps in front of Trinità dei Monti (with schemes that, at times, on a typological level, refer to villas), and even Giuseppe Valadier's projects for access from the Piazza del Popolo (executed 1816–20). The main features of the garden of the Villa Medici are derived, however, from two models of antiquity that were extant or reconstructable in the urban area between the Campus Martius and the Pincian: the "circus" space and the mausoleum.

That the area of garden on the axis of the palace may be interpreted as a "hippodrome" or "circus" is indicated by the obelisk erected by the engineer Camillo Agrippa in 1583–84 (that is, before the monuments erected by Sixtus V). The garden's layout may be related to the amphitheater of the Boboli Gardens in Florence; to the hippodrome in the gardens of Sallust; or to the supposed Circus of Flora, reconstructed by the Renaissance antiquaries in the area of the Quirinal. At the same time, on another hill of Rome, the Caelian, the "circus" of the Villa Mattei Celimontana was being constructed.

The mound of Parnassus in the Villa Medici, constructed between 1576 and 1583 on the remains of the Temple of Fortune, recalls a motif frequently proposed in sixteenth-century villas, from the Parnassus at the Villa Pratolino, north of Florence, to the various fountains of Pegasus. Equally, with its arrangement in descending rings crowned by cypresses, it is obviously modeled on the most famous mausoleum of ancient Rome, that of Augustus, which in the sixteenth century had been transformed by the Soderini family into a circular garden. The reference to the mausoleum in the Campus Martius (modeled on the burial mounds of the Etruscans, the precursors of Medicean rule) was light-heartedly confirmed by an inscription on the Parnassus mound comparing the engineering work of Camillo Agrippa to the schemes of Marcus Vipsanius Agrippa in the Campus Martius.

Another indication of the association between the Parnassus and the Mausoleum of Augustus is provided by the axial link of the Parnassus with the obelisk, which, in a way, recalls the two obelisks erected in antiquity in front of the mausoleum. As a mountain sacred to Apollo and the Muses, the Parnassus appears to be aligned with the solar symbolism that may also be identified with the Mausoleum of Augustus and the other solar monument in the Campus Martius, the Solarium Augusti.

The existence of a mausoleum/burial mound at the Villa Medici echoes the siting of Augustus's tomb: his mausoleum was surrounded by places suitable for promenading and gardens or *silvae* (woods) that in the Middle Ages were given the Greek name of "paradise." Indeed, the whole of the Campus Martius, according to a famous description by Strabo, was a sort of garden city; furthermore, it should be recalled that in antiquity the term *hortuli* was used to refer specifically to gardens around tombs. The supposed existence of another tomb structure should also be noted: some Renaissance antiquaries believed this was the site of Nero's Tomb, corresponding to the Mausoleum of the Domitians, the base of which was identified by Ligorio with the Muro Torto. The palace of Cardinal Ferdinando was thus situated within an imaginary triangle of three funerary structures: the true Mausoleum of Augustus, the supposed tomb of Nero, and the burial mound of Parnassus.

On another side of the Collis Hortulorum, in the area of the gardens of Sallust, the layout of the casino (now the Casino of the Aurora Ludovisi), built between 1575 and 1577 by Cecchino del Nero, appears to be analogous. The plan of this unusual building is a Greek cross, a cruciform formed by two axes oriented similarly to those of the Villa Medici. Since the patron's father, the Florentine Francesco del Nero, was a creature of the Medici, we can suppose that this parallel was intentional. Particularly important was the longitudinal axis forming the basis of the remarkable panoramic function of the casino. Placed on a hill described as a *belvedere* (vantage point), this axis pointed not only in the direction of two great ancient monuments, the Column of Antonius Pius and the Pantheon, but also toward another panoramic terrace of the Janiculum, that of San Pietro in Montorio.

In 1622 the casino became one of the nuclei of the immense Villa Ludovisi (fig. 11), created by combining four vineyards.[23] Particular prominence was given to the Palazzo Grande (formerly Palazzo degli Orsini) in front of which were twin labyrinthine *boschetti* (small wooded areas) adorned with statues. Laid out by the classicist painter Domenichino, the gardens seem to herald some of André Le Nôtre's schemes at Versailles. The guides recorded the antiquarian curiosities of the *boschetti*:

> There are a strange Egyptian idol, splendid figures of consuls, two barbarian prisoners with their hands tied, the handsome Silenus sleeping on an ancient urn adorned with the bas-relief of a battle, the group of a satyr with a small faun, a statue of Leda, twenty-six rare busts of emperors, and a splendid statue of Nero in a sacrificial robe.[24]

Aside from its labyrinthine museum and spectacular collections of statues (including the legendary Ludovisi Collection, now in the Museo Nazionale Romano), the villa was notable for the way its long shady paths fanned out systematically toward colossal antique statues, each framed against the backdrop of the Aurelian walls, which also constituted the boundary wall of the villa. Regrettably, the villa was largely obliterated by property speculation after 1885 (the only surviving buildings are the Casino dell'Aurora and part of the Palazzo Grande, incorporated into the Palazzo Margherita, now the American embassy). The poignancy of Gabriele d'Annunzio's description is still evident today:

> It seemed as if the wind of barbarism were blowing over Rome and threatening to tear away this radiant crown of patrician villas from it. . . . The trees lay on the ground next to each other, with all their roots exposed from which smoke rose toward the pale sky . . . while all around, on the splendid lawns where, the previous spring, the violets had, for the last time, appeared to be more numerous than the blades of grass, there were white puddles of lime and red heaps of bricks.[25]

The Rebirth of the Hills in the Sixteenth Century and the Primacy of the Quirinal

Parallel to developments on the Pincian Hill, from the fifteenth century onward the Quirinal became the hill of study and reflection on antiquity, nourished by the vision of the great architectural monuments, colossal statues like the Dioscuri of Monte Cavallo, and continuous discoveries of sculptures and other antiquities.[26] On the slopes of the Quirinal, the garden of the Colonna was laid out around the colossal ruins of the Temple of the Sun. At the end of the fifteenth century, Pomponio Leto established in his vineyard an academy that was both Platonic and Florentine in style for the study of antiquities and Roman history. From 1483 on, the foundation of Rome was once again celebrated here. At the beginning of the sixteenth century, on the site of the present Palazzo del Quirinale was the vineyard of Oliviero Carafa. It was rented in the middle of the century to Cardinal Ippolito d'Este, who, advised by Pirro Ligorio, built up an outstanding collection of statues there. But the most important "garden of statues" was without doubt the villa of Rodolfo Pio da

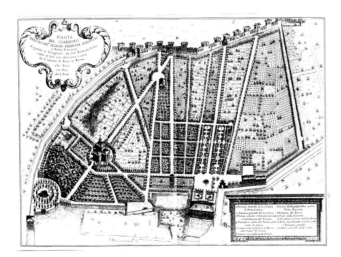

11. Villa Ludovisi (engraving by G. B. Falda, 1676). On the left is the area of Cecchino del Nero's casino in the shape of a Greek cross; at the bottom center is the Palazzo Grande; and above is the boundary wall formed by the Aurelian walls, where the main paths of the villa terminate with perspective backdrops.

Carpi, a cardinal from 1536 to 1564, whose villa was subsequently acquired by the Sforza and Barberini families. It is likely that Paul III (pope 1534–49) seriously considered the idea of setting up a residence on the Quirinal, but it was Pius IV who took the first steps toward a complete revival of the Quirinal and the other hills as an area for residential development in Rome, regarding himself as a new Augustus (who, on the contrary, had reclaimed the marshes of the Campus Martius in order to escape from the impasse of the seven hills).[27]

The principal axis of the development was to be the Via Pia (now Via del Quirinale and Via XX Settembre), the long straight road leading from the Quirinal to the backdrop of Michelangelo's Porta Pia, apparently a mere urban stage-set intended to enhance an area rich in sumptuous villas. Porta Pia was itself conceived as the gateway to a vineyard or garden. Moreover, this gate marked the edge of an area that was in the process of being transformed from agricultural land into an area of suburban villas. Derived from the rustic gateway type, the gate in turn influenced the design of various villa gateways, including that of the Farnese Gardens, completed by Jacopo del Duca, a pupil of Michelangelo who worked as a stonemason on the Porta Pia. In particular, the Porta Pia served as a model that architects commissioned to design rustic vineyard gateways along the Via Pia would have to take into account. The gateway of Pio da Carpi's gardens was surmounted by a cartouche culminating in a trapezoidal pediment evidently derived from the arch of Porta Pia. Elements originating from Michelangelo and del Duca are also present in the gateway of the Villa Caetani Sermoneta and the gateway of the Vigna Panzani, now in the Museo delle Terme, which includes both the trapezoidal arch motif and an open attic forming a window derived from the Farnese Gardens.

The beneficiaries of the improvement of the Quirinal were mainly associated with the pope, who, with his vineyard (between Monte Cavallo and Magnanapoli), himself joined this academy of the chosen few. On one side of the road were the properties of

Ippolito d'Este; the patriarch of Aquileia, Domenico Grimani; the cardinal of Carpi; and the Caetani. On the other side, after the Ferreri, Croce, Bandini, and Gherardi vineyards, came the largest property, the gardens of the cardinal Du Bellay, situated more or less on the site of Diocletian's palace, opposite his baths. The villa must have been particularly close to the heart of Pius IV, who acquired it in 1560 for his nephew Carlo Borromeo. Indeed, it is likely that the greatest incentive for the building of the road was the need for a link between the various residences, and also with Du Bellay's gardens. Sixtus V (originally Felice Peretti, pope 1585–90) continued Pius IV's plan with the interminable Via Felice (now Via Sistina, Via Quattro Fontane, Via Depretis, and Via Carlo Alberto), leading in a straight line from Trinità dei Monti to Santa Croce in Gerusalemme, intersecting the Via Pia at the crossroads of the Quattro Fontane.[28]

Due both to links with antiquity and to the shared desire of patrons to promote their public images, there are close affinities among the properties of the Via Pia. It is no coincidence that in the central section of the street, near the church of Santa Maria Maggiore, stood the villa that Sixtus had begun to build when he was a cardinal, extending it through later acquisitions of land. The main function of the Via Felice was, therefore, to serve Sixtus's villa. The casino was built by Domenico Fontana between 1578 and 1581—that is, in the same period as the Casino del Nero–Ludoviso, to which it was typologically similar due to the almost cruciform layout and the *altana* (covered roof terrace) in the form of a stepped tower. The main axis of the villa—comprising the casino and the belvedere on the Servian Walls, described as *altissimus Romae locus* or the highest place in Rome—pointed toward the center of Rome and the slopes of the Capitoline Hill. The villa was the Monte Alto to which Cardinal Peretti retreated, dominating the city from the *altana* of the casino, which was intended to be vaguely similar to the mythical tower of Maecenas (reconstructed by Pirro Ligorio as a stepped tower). According to Fontana, the pope wanted to build a palace-cum-observatory on the small hill of the Servian agger (the mound forming a rampart), sometimes identified as the site of Maecenas's tower, from where, according to legend, Nero watched the fire of Rome and planned the city's reconstruction. This is, however, also thought to be the location of the colossal statue of the goddess Roma (now in the Castello Massimo at Arsoli). There was an analogy with the other colossal statue of Roma, in the Villa Medici, originally placed in the garden facing toward the Vatican.

The complete revival of the hills would not have been possible without the construction of aqueducts to supply water not only for domestic and agricultural use but for public ornament in an area where, in antiquity, there had been a remarkable concentration of cisterns, reservoirs, colossal structures such as the baths, and displays and "castles" of water such as the "Trophies of Marius." Gregory XIII, favoring the new papal palace on the Quirinal Hill (fig. 12), decided in 1583 to build the aqueduct that was to be called Acqua Felice in honor of Sixtus V. The aqueduct was completed in December 1586. After a lull of more than a thousand years, an abundance of pure water allowed the creation of new public fountains, such as the one near the Baths of Diocletian. In the tradition lasting from the "Trophies of Marius" to the *nymphaea* in the mannerist and baroque gardens, the Moses Fountain is both a "castle" and a "theater of water": it is a triumphal arch welcoming the return of the water and a personal monument to the pope who, like Moses and Peter, performed the miracle of striking water from the rock.

In the center of the great cross formed by the Via Pia and Via Felice, the Quattro Fontane became the crossroads of a virtual garden city in an area that was in fact occupied by villas and vineyards. The layout of the octagonal space appears to echo the octagonal sculpture courtyard in the Belvedere Court, with four corner niches housing *Apollo*, *Venus Felix*, *Tigris*, and *Cleopatra*. Thus the four small *nymphaea* project toward passersby the myths and rites of a display of water that frames fascinating urban backdrops: the Porta Pia, the Sistine obelisk of Santa Maria Maggiore, the Dioscuri and the Sistine Fountain of the Quirinal,

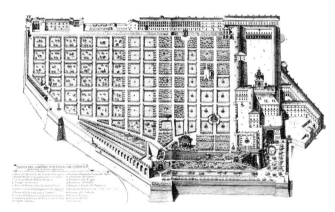

12. The papal gardens of the Quirinale (engraving by G. B. Falda, 1676). On the right is the Papal Palace dominated by the Torre dell'Orologio; below is the bastioned boundary wall of Urban VIII.

and the later obelisk of Pius VI at Trinità dei Monti. In a sense, the sculptural groups of the Quattro Fontane seek to qualify semantically the four sectors of the garden city: in the direction of the Esquiline are the river-gods Arno and Tiber, ordaining the twinning between Rome and Tuscany; toward Trinità dei Monti, Diana and Juno pay homage both to the ancient religions and the devices of the pope (*trimonzio*, or three hills, and lion). Each of the four compositions, with their natural-istic backgrounds (added after the mid-seventeenth century), is a representation of a *nymphaeum*, practically an altar consecrated to water.

The salubrity of the air and the amenity of the gardens induced Gregory XIII to build the second papal palace on the Quirinal Hill, beginning with the casino (designed by Ottaviano Mascarino), which was dominated by the Torre dei Venti (Tower of the Winds).[29] On the top of the hill, renowned for the way it dominated the city ("Colle Quirinali praestat qua miglior aura, vertice et sommo subdita Roma patet. . . ." [The Quirinal Hill rises where the air is mildest, and Rome spreads out below this noblest summit. . . .]), this tower-belvedere became the new vertex of the urban scene, joining the tower on the Capitoline Hill and corresponding to the other Torre dei Venti in the Vatican (also built by Gregory XIII). The eagerness to dominate the surrounding area is documented by a chronicler who attributed to the pope the intention "to dominate not only the seven hills, but also to descry its environs until the sea."[30]

Completed by Paul V (pope 1605–21), the palace-villa of the Quirinal was extended and trans-formed into a fortified citadel by Urban VIII (pope 1623–44). Under Alexander VII (pope 1655–67) the Quirinal very nearly became the center of the city when serious consideration was given to the idea of moving the court to the hill. With increasing frequency, the Quirinal served as the papal residence in the sev-enteenth and eighteenth centuries; in the Napoleonic period, it continued to evolve as a project for the cre-ation of an enormous palace. Until September 20, 1870, the palace hosted the most important acts of the government of Pius IX, the last pope before Rome and the Papal States were incorporated into Italy. When Rome was proclaimed the capital of Italy, the Quirinal became the palace of the Savoy kings and, subsequently, the residence of the president of the Italian Republic.

Large Villas outside the Walls: Antiquarian Culture and the Arcadian Landscape

At the beginning of the seventeenth century a tendency, together with the recurring antiquarian taste, to add increasingly large areas of agricultural land or unculti-vated countryside to the villa began to assert itself. This land was neither the formal garden nor the wood or *barco* (park) that appeared in Rome, for example, at the Vatican or outside the city at Bagnaia. The strategy followed by Domenico Fontana at the Villa Montalto (fig. 13) is significant:

> *Although a large sum of money has been spent in this enterprise, because the area was covered with hills and val-leys that were leveled and filled in to make the site flat, it is also true that, in some places, numerous gentle slopes and pleasant valleys have been left deliberately to make it more attractive.*[31]

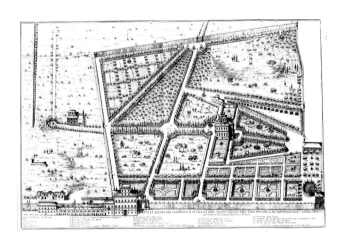

13. Villa Montalto (engraving by G. B. Falda, 1676).

It has been noted that the concept of landscape, as opposed to the formal garden,

> *represents the disturbing conflict between art and unspoiled nature, a reminiscence of the ancient Italic grove, heralding the new aesthetic of the picturesque garden. . . . The remnant of the Campagna of Rome that has been enclosed by the boundary wall finds its imaginary horizons in the outlines of the aqueducts and the archaeological remains emerging on the hill.[32]*

A new ideal of the classical landscape—both antiquarian and Arcadian—began to appear. In the decades following, it established itself especially in painting, first in the work of Carracci and Domenichino and then in that of Poussin and Lorraine. The two largest villas of the seventeenth century, the Borghese (figs. 14, 15) and the Doria Pamphili (figs. 16, 17), were built outside the walls, making it possible for their boundaries and prospects to be expanded, in a dual dialogue with the "satyric stage-set" of the woods, valleys, and heights, and with the "tragic stage-set" of the aqueducts, walls, and gates of Rome. Their sites were also similar, with the first villa located on a higher hill than the Pincian and Esquiline and the second on an offshoot of the Janiculum. The vastness of the estates allowed them to vie with the "rustic villas" of antiquity, which, according to Columella's famous treatise,[33] comprised three different sections: the *pars urbana* (the owner's residence with the adjoining garden); the pars *rustica* (the residence of the bailiff and slaves with the adjoining enclosures for the animals); and the *pars fructuaria* (area of cultivated land). In late Renaissance and early baroque garden theory, the contrast between the formal garden and the park was compared, paraphrasing Columella's classification, to the distinction between urban order (the formal garden was the *pars urbana* of the villa) and the disorder of the countryside (the analogy between the park and the *pars rustica*).

In the villa of Scipione Borghese, the omnipotent nephew of Paul V, the enclosed layout of the formal garden in front of and behind the casino-museum contrasted with the vaster expanse of the agricultural area, the boundaries of which "were lost in the rural landscape of the Campagna of Rome, which extended from Monte Mario to the hills of Rieti."[34] The seventeenth-century park of the Villa Borghese was described in 1650:

> *In the third and last enclosure of the villa, Nature has revealed herself in the unevenness of the site, because in her work she takes delight in being varied, and has also given an opportunity to Art to show her industry in the organization and orderly regulation of such a large space . . . that comprises within its vastness valleys, hills, plains, woods, houses, and gardens, thereby providing very convenient refuge for many animals of different species, such as hares, roe-deer, fallow deer, and other kinds of deer, peacocks, ducks, and other smaller birds, which may be seen running and flying freely in the countryside.[35]*

In contrast with the freedom of the park, the *pars urbana* took the form of a city in miniature, on the model of the Roman castrum, with the palace corresponding to the ancient praetorium[36] and a network of avenues consisting of five *cardines* (north-south streets) that intersect the *decumani* (east-west streets) orthogonally, as in the castra. The resemblance of the villa to the city is evident in a plan of the Villa Borghese of 1776 that describes the palace as the praetorium; the same name is given to the palace-museum of the Villa Albani in a similar classicizing plan of the previous year.[37]

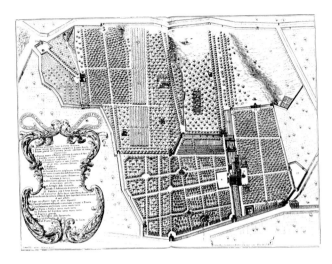

14. Villa Borghese (engraving by S. F. Delino, 1676). The view includes the seventeenth-century nucleus of the villa with its three enclosures: one at bottom center; one on the right—beyond the villa (now Galleria Borghese); and one at the top, the third and largest.

Aside from the facades of the palace adorned with antique statuary, other aspects of the villa reveal an archaeological influence. For instance, there were the colossal and majestic antique herms, recomposed and completed by Pietro Bernini with overflowing baskets of fruit, figures symbolizing the communion of man with the vegetable kingdom. Then there was the oval loggia or "small dining room"—a *cenatio* in the woods with a central plan, like the famous one in the Domus Aurea—with a fresco of the *Banquet of the Gods* on the ceiling and a device—inspired by the description of Nero's residence—that scattered perfumed flowers over the guests.[38] Contemporary accounts refer to a lawn in the shape of a circus, with a small granite obelisk at the center.[39] Thus, there was the "theater adorned with statues, marbles, and ancient

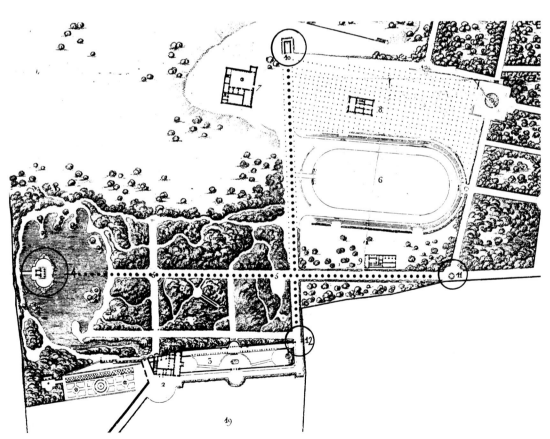

15. Plan of the late-eighteenth-century nucleus of Villa Borghese (engraving from Percier and Fontaine, 1824). The two most important avenues intersect and end in the perspective backdrops of the Temple of Faustina (10), the Temple of Diana (11), the bridge of the Acqua Felice (12), and the Temple of Aesculapius (4). Also shown are the circus or Piazza di Siena (6) and the entrance from the Muro Torto, which imitates the propylaea of Hadrian's villa (1).

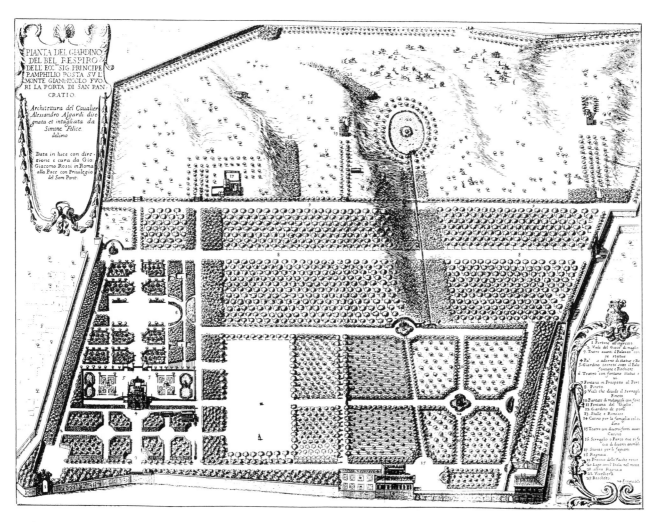

16. Plan of the seventeenth-century nucleus of Villa Doria
Pamphili (engraving by G. B. Falda, 1676).

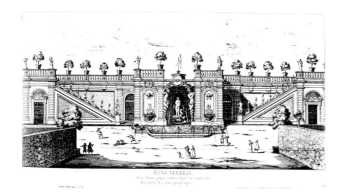

17. Villa Doria Pamphili (engraving by G. B. Falda, 1676). The Venus
Fountain is set into the retaining wall of the walled garden in front of
the villa.

inscriptions"—that is, the semicircular space enclosed by the architectural backdrop attributed to Girolamo Rainaldi (executed 1617–19). The aviaries are also attributed to Rainaldi, who designed those in the Farnese Gardens. Their facades are embellished with bas-reliefs and antique busts and are crowned by orientalizing transparent domed cages:

Inside they are painted with splendid views of gardens and the countryside, with small birds and festoons of flowers; in the center there are two fountains to water the birds, large numbers of which, of many different species, live in these delightful prisons.[40]

Several decades later, the other large suburban villa was built. It was commissioned by Camillo Pamphili, the young cardinal nephew of Innocent X (pope 1644–55), who renounced the cardinal's hat to marry Olimpia Aldobrandini in 1647. In 1644 and 1645 Camillo ordered projects from both Bernini (according to a recent study by C. Benocci) and Borromini, perhaps suggesting that they should make use of Serlian and Palladian models and draw on the great villas of antiquity such as the Domus Aurea and Hadrian's Villa. Drawings and an autograph account describe Borromini's project for a fortified casino, with four avant-corps in the form of bastions at the corners, in the center of a garden with capriccios and curiosities. The casino—in front of which there was a flight of steps in the form of a sundial recording the time and the day of the month—had thirty-two windows corresponding to the thirty-two winds,

and in two round rooms there could be a vault, which between them would form a celestial orb, where the stars could be painted as they are in the heavens, and perhaps on the model of the one Nero had built in his palace, they could be made to turn.[41]

In addition to this revival of the cosmological room of the Domus Aurea, Borromini suggested making a statue of the pope

placed in such a position that, on September 15, a ray of sunlight would kiss the statue's feet at the time when he was made pope; this practice was common among the ancients.

Other ideas that were considered included the flooding of paths and squares in order to allow the guests to have pleasure trips by boat, and the creation of a sort of Noah's Ark, a menagerie with cages for real animals or artificial ones.[42]

Evidently, neither Borromini nor Bernini was able to interpret the wishes of the patron, an amateur architect as well as a lover of literature, music, and theater. In the end, he engaged the services not of an architect but of a sculptor, Alessandro Algardi (appointed also because of his skill as a restorer of antique statuary), assisted by a landscape painter, the Bolognese Giovanni Francesco Grimaldi. As may be seen in the seventeenth-century plans, the villa was

subdivided into three parts: the pars rustica *with the menagerie occupying the southern part, the* pars urbana *or monumental part, and the* pars fructuaria. *Between the first part and the other two there was an intermediate area, where a pinewood was planted. The main linking element was a waterway that began in the agricultural part, where it fed various fountains; the canal ended in a "lake with an island in the middle" surrounded by tall trees; the water flowed into a smaller canal that crossed a* ragnaia [a *wood with nets to trap birds].*[43]

The *pars urbana* surrounded the *casino nobile* or the Casino del Belrespiro. Spectacularly embellished with antique statuary, its typology seemed to be a compromise between the Roman casinos with their statuary-adorned facades and cruciform or pseudo-cruciform plans (from the Villa Montalto to the Casino del Nero–Ludovisi) and the Palladian villas with their central rotundas. The remarkable decorative scheme has been interpreted as

the exaltation of the valor of the patrons and the famous characters of antiquity, in an imaginary continuation of the Pamphili family: the trophies, with Medusa's heads and the fleur-de-lis of the Pamphili on the capitals, are a reference to the family's military prowess, to which is added the heroic fury linked to the myth of Achilles and that of Hercules, the symbol of Renaissance and Baroque man, who rises to the divine sphere through the choice of virtue, a theme to which a whole room was devoted.[44]

Particular prominence is given to the axial garden in front, intersected by the orthogonal axis of the Theater Garden. The center of the composition still appears to be the exedra, a true theater of glory, love, and the arts, adorned with busts of emperors (the mythical ancestors of the Pamphili) and antique and modern reliefs with musical, erotic, and Dionysian scenes. One of the two rustic *nymphaea* (the one to the right of the "theater") remains; it is described as having

> *two sirens in the water, and a mascaron continuously spouting water in the form of an umbrella, adorned with a large number of stone dolphins: and directly in front of it are fountains, with basins made in the shape of candelabra, which spout water continuously and appear to be many candles illuminating this* nymphaeum.[45]

The key to the significance of the garden appears to be the Venus Fountain, inserted by Algardi in the retaining wall of the casino. The antiquarian and biographer Giovanni Pietro Bellori explains it thus:

> *He made the fountain of Venus, standing on a shell drawn by dolphins. . . . Amid the bas-relief stuccoes above in the vault there is a Cupid shooting an arrow. . . . On one side, in small ovals and statuettes, there are the four elements, personified by Jupiter, Juno, Cybele, and Amphitrite, opposite which another four figures of the seasons correspond, and all together they denote the power of Venus and the nature of the universe.*[46]

The whole scheme revolves around the iconography, deriving from Botticelli, of the birth of Venus from the waters. The allegory unites the force at the center of the universe with, on the one hand, the "Olympic"

wedding of the patron under the sign of Love the Conqueror and, on the other, the origin myths of the Pamphili, who were, according to legend, the descendants of Aeneas and therefore of his mother, Venus.

From Classicism to Eclecticism: An Overview of the History

Three works, realized outside Rome's walls between the mid-eighteenth and the mid-nineteenth centuries, express the intensity and complexity of the revival of antiquity: the Villa Albani on the Via Salaria, the rebuilding of the Villa Borghese by Antonio and Mario Asprucci and Luigi Canina, and the Villa Torlonia, the quintessence and apogee of eclecticism in Rome. The three works represent very different programs, devised for very dissimilar patrons: Cardinal Alessandro Albani; Prince Camillo Borghese, Napoleon's son-in-law; and Alessandro Torlonia, a newly created noble and a "Croesus of Rome."

The inspirer of Cardinal Albani's villa-museum[47] (figs. 18, 19), Johann Joachim Winckelmann, appears today to be the prime mover behind a new concept of "memory of the future closely linked to the expectation of the past, with the reversal of linear time in the ever-returning circularity of the neoclassical ideal of antiquity as future."[48] His unconditional adherence may be deduced from a number of passages in his letters, where he describes an astounding dream inspired by antiquity:

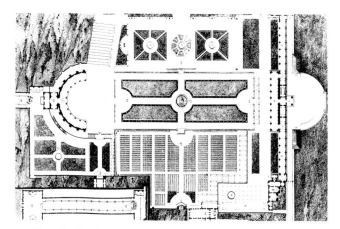

18. Plan of Villa Albani (engraving from Percier and Fontaine, 1824).

19. The casino-museum at Villa Albani (engraving by G. Vasi, 1761).

The cardinal is the man who is carrying out the most astonishing work in Rome. . . . His villa surpasses anything else that has been built in Rome in modern times, except for the basilica of St. Peter's. . . . The villa will prove to be as we imagine the Capitol Hill in antiquity.[49]

In fact, the villa must have appeared to be a basilica, citadel, theater, and museum of antiquity, in a new hill of the muses emulating the ancient and modern glories of the Vatican and Capitoline Hill.[50]

Aside from the first garden with a radial layout, adjacent to the Via Salaria, the villa is particularly notable for the neo-sixteenth-century space in the form of a court between the palace and the semicircular arcade of the Coffeehouse, beyond which the watercourse of the Euripus formerly extended with its seven small waterfalls. Another fascinating feature is the "Temple of Jupiter," apparently a ruin:

This false ruin, constructed with authentic remains, forms part of that current of eighteenth-century antiquarianism that permitted the integrative and arbitrary restoration of ancient statues. The descriptive accuracy of the ruin and the quasi-theatrical setting recalls Pannini's capriccios with their evocative, make-believe architecture. Since Roman ruins were visible in many important Roman villas of the sixteenth century, Cardinal Albani also wanted to enjoy a view of a "ruined building."[51]

From a typological point of view the villa derives from the combination of models of the villa-museum and real museums. While, as regards the former, there are evident affinities with the sixteenth-century villas *all'antica*, such as the Villa Madama, the similarity with the intermediate type of the villa-theater should be stressed. This derives from the hippodrome of Pliny the Younger's Tuscan villa, which inspired the

Belvedere Court and the "circus" of the Villa Mattei Celimontana. The prototypes of the "museum" include the Casino of Pius IV and the Villa Medici, as well as the buildings on the Capitoline Hill, especially the "Palazzo Nuovo," built in the mid-seventeenth century to house a museum. Thus the long arcade of the Villa Albani is derived from the Capitoline palaces (which more evidently inspired the initial project, outlined by Giovanni Battista Nolli).[52] It should also be noted that the Belvedere Court, the first example of a villa-museum, was completed, perhaps on the model of the Villa Albani, with the Braccio Nuovo (new wing) built by Raffaele Stern in 1817–22 (part of the Museo Chiaramonti). Leaving aside these typological considerations, however, the fascination of the Villa Albani lies wholly in the relationship between the garden, antiquity, and the landscape. The villa has been described as

> an archaeological park, which was intended to bring the ancient world back to life in natural surroundings: in this identification of antiquity with nature the aim was to recover the original coincidence of happiness and virtue that had been lost with the end of the ancient world. . . . The antique statuary, the arrangement of which was supervised by Winckelmann in person, formed a single display, reflecting the unity of antiquity and nature.[53]

The work carried out at the end of the eighteenth century by Prince Marc'Antonio Borghese on the western part of his villa (1776–93, under the supervision of the architects Antonio and Mario Asprucci) was evidently influenced by, on the one hand, the Villa Albani and, on the other, the tradition of the English landscaped garden (crossed with the wide straight approaches and long views typical of Italian and French gardens). On an islet in the middle of a romantic lake with sinuous banks stood the Temple of Aesculapius, evidently based on the sanctuary of Aesculapius on the Isola Tiberina. A number of the most important buildings were placed like stage backdrops at the four ends of a cross of avenues that, due to the effect of perspective, recalls the urban crossroads

of the Quattro Fontane. On the main axis, the Temple of Aesculapius faces the circular Tempietto of Diana-Luna (dedicated to the Noctilucae Silvarum Potenti, or powerful nocturnal goddess of the woods). On the transverse axis the Tempietto of Faustina—a sham ruin built with a medley of antique elements, imitating the one at the Villa Albani—faces the gate-bridge of the Acqua Felice (destroyed by the French cannonade in 1849). The Piazza di Siena pays homage only nominally to the medieval square in the city of the Borghese family's origin where the famous *palio* takes place; in reality, it was designed to be a circus *all'antica*, with a central spina.[54]

In the nineteenth-century rebuilding of the Villa Borghese (carried out by Camillo Borghese, son of Marc'Antonio)[55] and the Villa Torlonia (commissioned by Alessandro Torlonia),[56] the desire to recreate the model of the villa *all'antica* par excellence, Hadrian's Villa, symbolizing eclecticism and universalism, is quite explicit. For example, Luigi Canina wrote that the Villa Borghese, renewed by the Asprucci and himself,

> was more similar than any other to Hadrian's famous villa at Tivoli, and just as this comprised the Lyceum, the Academy, the Prytaneum, Canopus, the Stoa Poikile, Tempe, and the places of the future life, this includes a magnificent palace with other smaller ones, a fortress, a hippodrome, and various temples imitating the buildings of antiquity; indeed the Villa Borghese, as rebuilt by Asprucci, has its entrance decorated in the same style as that of Hadrian's Villa.[57]

The idea that inspired the great complex of the Villa Torlonia (figs. 20–22) is very similar:

> On seeing this magnificent scene, these monuments that dominate the solitude of the pleasant countryside, the astonished spectator will say to himself: certainly only a great and noble lord would be able to procure these supreme delights. And the architect worked well because, at a glance, he could enjoy the product of his greatness. Just as Hadrian was pleased that, from one point in his villa, he

could observe all the monuments in various styles that, thanks to his powerful will, he had collected; so Caretti, when conceiving the principal view of the villa, worked in such a way that, as far as the site would permit, many varied monuments could be seen from a single viewpoint; thus, their lord could command an excellent view of them all in an instant.[58]

20. View from the boundary wall of Villa Torlonia (engraving by G. B. Caretti, from G. Checchetelli, 1842).

In fact, in 1822 the visual and scenographic requirements received a great deal of attention in the debate over the reorganization of the Villa Borghese and the renewal of the monumental entrance to Rome through the important road junction of Porta and Piazza del Popolo. Giuseppe Valadier, who at that time was directing the work on the piazza and the Pincian, suggested linking Asprucci's propylaea to Piazza del Popolo by a rectilinear avenue that would have involved the partial demolition of the Muro Torto. In Canina's more ambitious project, the problem of access was linked to the reorganization of the area toward the Via Flaminia, in full accord with the proposals of his rival Valadier. The rectilinear avenue leading to the Greek propylaea employed the traditional schema of the straight road and the scenographic view both toward the old nucleus of the villa and toward the city, the Tiber, and St. Peter's. ("The magnificent Vatican building is almost in the direction of the main road," Canina wrote.[59]) From the hexagonal junction halfway along the avenue, traffic could reach the two new entrances to the original nucleus of the villa, near to the two bridges over the old boundary road. In the center of the junction, the fountain of Aesculapius, with the triumph of wild, cragged nature, was also the introduction to the triumph of historical memory, after the Greek revival of the classical propylaea and before the revival of Rome (the Arch of Septimius Severus) and the ancient East (the Egyptian propylaea).

Aside from the functional choice of the different historical models, even within the same historical area Canina carried out audacious combinations of forms. Thus the classical propylaea were derived from a critical analysis of the various propylaea of Athens, Eleusis, Priene, the temple of the Athena of Sunium, and the Portico of Octavia in Rome. The final result corresponded to

the form in parastades of the propylaea of Sunium . . . reducing their length—that is, bringing the two fronts closer together, on the model of the above-mentioned Portico of Octavia, to allow part of the pleasant view of the villa to be more easily visible between the columns.[60]

The choice of the Ionic order, the traditional intermediary "between the Doric solidity and the great ornateness of the Corinthian," appears to be derived from the propylaea of the enclosure of the Athena Polias at Preine due to the singular combination of capitals in different styles under the same architrave.

Canina justified the presence of the Egyptian propylaea because they met the demand for eclecticism ("in order to give the new buildings a more varied appearance") and because they served as a parallel to the references to ancient Egypt present in Hadrian's Villa. Even the choice of a reduction in scale compared with the eastern model can be traced back to a similar choice by the emperor-architect. On the other hand, the elimination of the pedestal in the obelisks—which, unlike the Roman examples, rose directly from the ground—echoed Egyptian practice. It should be noted that these two obelisks were the first to be constructed and erected in post-classical Rome in imitation of the antique models. In fact, they were built with bricks covered in stucco to simulate granite and, for the first time—fifteen years before the obelisks of Torlonia—a hieroglyphic inscription was devised (in honor of the patron, with the advice of the archaeologist Sir William Gell), thus making good use of the recent discoveries in Egyptian writing.

Even the apparently unexceptional triumphal arch, dedicated to Septimius Severus, is worthy of mention for its role as a historical memento (in fact, an honorary monument to Septimius Severus stood nearby) and for its experimentation with a mixture of styles and degrees of artistic license. The construction is modeled on the proportions and dimensions of the Arch of Titus and reproduces the inscription on the Arch of the Argentari (money-changers). However,

> the columns that are commonly to be found in the arches of the ancients have been omitted because their use in this case would be contrary to their normal use, and they would be only decorative here. Above the cornice, the large attic used by the ancients in these cases for the inscriptions was not built, because often this makes the construction appear ungainly.[61]

Thus the addition to the Villa Borghese was both an opportunity for experimentation and a theater for the phantoms of history. The evocation of further proposals has remained on paper:

> On this hill it would be fitting to build in the middle a temple with ancient architecture similar to those that were constructed on the Acropolis of the city of the Greeks. . . . The ridge of the hill facing the Via Flaminia has a suitable position; here, with great facility, it would be possible to create the tiers of seats of a theater in a similar manner to that of the ancient Greeks, or rather in imitation of those erected at the foot of the rock of Athens.[62]

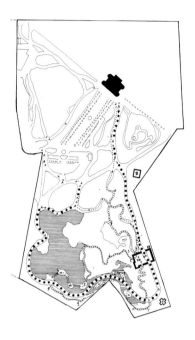

The ghost of the Acropolis dissolves, therefore, into the wraith of a coruscating Middle Age:

> During the restoration of the two houses, which are in the area of this extension, they will be decorated with merlons and other ornaments in medieval style, although their picturesque forms will be maintained. In this way, the Borghese Gardens will be enriched with buildings, constructed in the manner used by various peoples of the past.[63]

Perhaps because of its much smaller size, the Villa Torlonia has a more spectacular concentration of architectural forms, techniques, and building types. The villa was conceived as a series of wonders, in the tradition extending from Hadrian's Villa to the creations of the architect Giuseppe Jappelli (who designed the garden of the Villa Torlonia) passing metaphorically through the hell and purgatory of the Sacro Bosco at Bomarzo, in northern Lazio. The villa constituted a compendium of knowledge, symbolizing the frenetic thirst for action and learning of the Torlonia.

The Via Nomentana was overlooked by a colossal stage-set, partly sham, for the performances of the court and Roman society. It was all ostentation: everything was arranged so that people could watch others and, at the same time, show themselves off. The official views stress the character of the artificial landscape constructed as a backdrop, to be seen at a glance. With the various buildings standing out on the horizon, the villa took on the appearance of a *veduta ideata*, combining the sense of déja vu in its individual elements with the capriccio in the assemblage of the pieces. The villa was, in effect, a panorama—or diorama—thanks to the simultaneous presence of history on the stage and nature in the background, and through the leveling of past and present. Giovanni Battista Caretti's taste for the picturesque was com-

21. Project by G. Jappelli for the layout of the garden at Villa Torlonia (from a drawing in the Museo Civico in Padua, revised by M. Fagiolo). The lake and the two main avenues, used by carriages and travelers on horseback, have been highlighted.

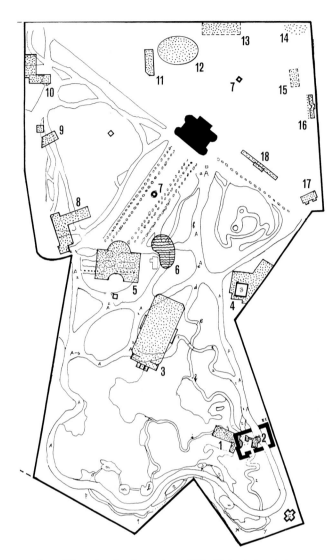

22. Jappelli's project for the garden at Villa Torlonia in relation to the main buildings of the villa (drawing by M. Fagiolo). Shown are the Moorish greenhouse (1), Moorish tower (2), tournament field (3), Swiss cabin (4), theater and orangery (5), small lake alluding to Lake Fucino (6), obelisks (7), *limonaia* and cottage in medieval style (8), new stables (9), old stables (10), small palace of the prince (11), amphitheater (12), ruins of the Temple of Minerva (13), ruins of an amphitheater (14), coffeehouse (15), ruins of baths (16), Temple of Saturn (17), and tribune and fountain (18).

pleted by Jappelli with his mediation between the scenography and spectacularity.

If ancient Rome was the city "where the arts were magnificently displayed in all their greatness, was the palace of the universe,"[64] the villa in its turn seemed to proclaim itself a compendium of ancient Rome. Contemporary critics could thus extol the "revival of a spectacle that had not been seen since the reign of the emperor Constantius II, the arrival on the banks of the regal Tiber of obelisks."[65] But, although the importation of monoliths from Baveno on Lake Maggiore had a neo-imperial flavor, and their erection in the villa was obviously intended to emulate the papal strategy, these antecedents were concealed by the more evident presence of a commemorative function: they were dedicated to Alessandro's parents, the founders of the financial empire of the Torlonia. The extraordinary spectacle of the erection of the obelisks was the dress rehearsal for the scenic potential of the villa. The technology applied (mechanical contrivances of various kinds) became a spectacle of science and technology, a tangible sign of the omnipotence of the prince, and the traditional curiosity of the people was supplemented by the expectations of the upper classes and the foreigners, attracted by the promise that they would be able to watch a cultural, almost sacred rite.

The poetry of the ancient world and ruins—although, as in the Villa Albani and Villa Borghese, here too the ruins are fake—is expressed didactically in the pediment of the Temple of Saturn, sculpted by Vincenzo Gaiassi with an allegory of human existence and Time triumphing over Joy, Art, and Culture:

> *which is intent, with the harmony of music, on soothing the pains of the heart, which abandons itself to pleasure and finally seeks relief from itself in the arts and science: in the middle, Father Time rises above them all, as if he were their master. In his hands he has a scythe; soon he will swing it and they will disappear before him, just as they disappeared the other times.*[66]

The symphony of Time becomes its exorcism on the part of the lord of the place:

> Oh, the architect of these delights did well to erect an altar to that destructive numen! Oh, thanks to this votive offering may he be tardy in swinging his scythe against these places in order to make them return to nothing! May he not aspire to erect a temple on their ruins, while a truly noble one may be erected to his power by their master.[67]

The lord and father of the arts was thus placed under the protection of Father Time, who

> lives in this place and rules in the past, present, and future, so that the glories of Alessandro Torlonia, father of the fine arts, shall not sink into oblivion.[68]

In the cavalcade of time, the villa was also placed under the sign of Ludovico Ariosto and Torquato Tasso—that is, of chivalrous fantasy and melancholy. In contrast to the popular games of the Roman plebeians and the spectacles of the papal court, the newly created aristocrat Torlonia did not hesitate to organize tournaments in order to give his freshly won nobility a medieval and Renaissance patina. Thus he commissioned Jappelli to create a tournament field so that the "noble youth may be invigorated by taking part in jousts."

More interesting, perhaps, are the "marvels" or "surprises" devised by Jappelli, with celebrated examples of mobile architecture. In the Sala della Torre Moresca could be seen

> various chairs covered with fine damask and a large round one in the middle. But is this the truth that I see or deception? It rises up to the dome of the room forming a canopy, and its place is taken by a table, which can be prepared for a banquet in the kitchen below: this is a joyous new demonstration of magnificence and ingenuity.[69]

Once again, this seems to resemble the rotating room of the Domus Aurea. In the adjacent Serra Moresca, a true theatrical space, at a nod from the master the end wall disappeared "to reveal an arched room, to be used by the orchestra on any festive occasion."[70] One might say that the architect's conjuring tricks were in harmony with the great financial operations or even the political evolution of the Torlonia—not, perhaps, without ironic undertones.

The counterpart of the Triumph of Time was the Triumph of Mother Nature, celebrated in the mysterious sacrarium of the grotto, now unfortunately destroyed. It was linked to the maternal elements of the earth and water and dedicated to the guardian nymphs of the place. In the route planned by Jappelli, guests entered and exited the grotto twice, with a hermetic ritual of conception, death, and birth, accompanied by the trickling of water and the pattern of light and shade:

> How vast is this solitude! What a contrast its natural darkness forms with the bright sky that, appearing through a number of holes, disperses it with its light![71]

Solitude involves cancellation; the return to Mother Nature occasions an antenatal aura: "Silence reigns here: art seems not to have been adopted at all."[72] But the place must have had the subterranean force of both the kingdom of Hades and primeval nature: the only signs of life were the grasses that "with their green color, although sad, seem to stress that the vitality of nature exists everywhere, even underground."[73]

Acknowledgments

The entries on the Chigi Farnesina, Lante on the Janiculum, Ludovisi, Doria Pamphili, and Chigi villas are by Mario Bevilacqua.

The authors would like to thank Dottoressa Anna Capuzzi and the owners of the villas whose kind cooperation facilitated the work of the photographer.

Notes

1. For an overview of the villas of Rome the monograph by I. Belli Barsali, *Ville di Roma*, 2nd ed. (Milan, 1983) is fundamental. See also D. Coffin, *The Villa in the Life of Renaissance Rome* (Princeton, 1979); A. Tagliolini, *Storia del giardino italiano* (Florence, 1988); M. Fagiolo, *Roma delle delizie. I teatri dell'acqua: grotte, ninfei, fontane* (Milan, 1990); and D. Coffin, *Gardens and Gardening in Papal Rome* (Princeton, 1991).

2. E. La Rocca, "Il lusso come espressione di potere," in M. Cima and E. La Rocca, *Le tranquille dimore degli Dei* (Rome, 1986), 7. For the gardens of Rome, see P. Grimal, *Les jardins romains* (Paris, 1944; 3rd ed., Paris, 1984).

3. Vitruvius, *De architectura*, IV, 5, 2.

4. Seutonius, *De vita Caesarum*, VI, 31.

5. Tacitus, *Annales*, XVI, 42.

6. Seutonius, *De vita Caesarum*, VI, 39.

7. Seutonius, *De vita Caesarum*, VI, 31.

8. Seutonius, *De vita Caesarum*, VI, 31.

9. H. P. l'Orange, "Domus aurea . . . der Sonnenpalast," in *Serta Eitremiana* (Oslo, 1942), 68–100; H. P. l'Orange, *Studies on the Iconography of Cosmic Kingship in the Ancient World* (Oslo, 1953). For the symbolism of the cosmic dome see also K. Lehmann, "The Dome of Heaven," in *Art Bulletin* (1945): 21–22; L. Hautecoeur, *Mystique et architecture: Symbolisme du cercle et de la coupole* (Paris, 1954); and E. B. Smith, *The Dome: Architectural Symbolism of Imperial Rome and the Middle Age* (Princeton, 1956). More recently the cosmic room of the Domus Aurea has been linked not only to the *aviarium* described by Varro, but also to the Maritime Theater in Hadrian's Villa, for which a rotating cosmic dome has been hypothesized. See H. Stierlin, *Hadrien et l'architecture romaine* (Fribourg, 1984).

10. Lucan, *De bello civili*, I, 45.

11. For the Vatican gardens see D. Redig de Campos, *I Palazzi Vaticani* (Bologna, 1967); E. Schröter, "Der Vatikan als Hügel Apollons und der Musen: Kunst und Panegyrik von Nikolaus V bis Julius II," in *Römisches Quartalschrift* (1980): 208–40; C. Pietrangeli and F. Manicelli, eds., *Vaticano: città e giardini* (Vatican, 1985); G. Morello, A. M. Piazzoni, and E. Young, *I Giardini del Vaticano* (Rome, 1991); and C. Pietrangeli, ed., *Il Palazzo Apostolico Vaticano* (Florence, 1992). See also my subsequent studies (and the biographical notes contained in them): "Dai palazzi ai giardini," in M. Fagiolo, *L'arte dei papi* (Milan, 1982), 188–211.

12. J. S. Ackerman, *The Cortile del Belvedere* (Vatican, 1954); A. Bruschi, *Bramante architetto* (Bari, 1969). See also A. Guarna, *Scimmia*, ed. E. Battisti (Rome, 1970).

13. See especially M. Fagiolo and M. L. Madonna, "La Casina di Pio IV in Vaticano," in *Storia dell'arte* 15–16 (1972): 237–81; M. Fagiolo and M. L. Madonna, "La Roma di Pio IV," in *Arte Illustrata* (1972): 383–402, and *Arte Illustrata* (1973): 186–212; and G. Smith, *The Casino of Pius IV* (Princeton, 1977).

14. For the villa see R. Lefevre, *Villa Madama* (Rome, 1973); S. Ray, *Raffaello Architetto* (Rome and Bari, 1974); J. Shearman, "A Functional Interpretation of Villa Madama," in *Römisches Jahrbuch für Kunstgeschichte* (1983): 221–40; and C. L. Frommel, S. Ray, and M. Tafuri, *Raffaello Architetto* (Milan, 1984); and C. L. Frommel, "Living *all'antica*: Palaces and Villas from Brunelleschi to Bramante," in *The Renaissance from Brunelleschi to Michelangelo*, ed. H. Millon and V. Magnago Lampugnani (exhibition catalog, Milan, 1994), 183–203.

15. For the Villa Giulia see especially J. Coolidge, "The Villa Giulia," in *Art Bulletin* (1943): 177–225; T. Falk, "Studien zur Topographie und der Geschichte der Villa Giulia in Rom," in *Römisches Jahrbuch für Kunstgeschichte* (1971): 101–78; C. Davis, "Villa Giulia e la fontana dell'Acqua Vergine," in *Psicon* 8–9 (1976); and T. Carunchio et al., "Villa Giulia: Un caso esemplare della cultura e della prassi costruttiva nella metà del Cinquecento," in *Bollettino d'Arte* (March–April 1987): 47–97.

16. See especially H. Giess, "Studien zur Farnese-Villa am Palatin," in *Römisches Jahrbuch für Kunstgeschichte* (1971): 179–229; and two volumes of conference proceedings devoted to the gardens: *Gli Horti Farnesiani sul Palatino: Giardino, storia e conservazione* (Rome, 1985), especially M. Fagiolo, "Idea degli Horti Farnesiani. 'Roma quadrata' e il 'Foro della Pace' "; and *Gli Horti Farnesiani* (Rome, 1990).

17. The origin of the Farnese Gardens has been correctly associated with Charles V's triumphal entry into Rome in 1536. See M. L. Madonna, "L'ingresso di Carlo V a Roma," in M. Fagiolo, *La città effimera e l'universo artificiale del giardino* (Rome, 1980), 63–68.

18. Giess, "Studien zur Farnese-Villa," 182.

19. L. Fauno, *Delle antichità della città di Roma* (Venice, 1553), 65.

20. See M. Fagiolo, "Archetipologie degli Horti Farnesiani," in *Gli Horti Farnesiani*, 245–51.

21. From the report of 1811 (Louvre archives), quoted by O. Poisson, "Foro e Palatino, 1809–13: Il progetto del Giardino del Campidoglio," in *Gli Horti Farnesiani*, 587–603. See also A. Lapadula, *Roma e la regione nell'età napoleonica* (Rome, 1959).

22. For the villa and its gardens, see G. Andrès, "The Villa Medici" (doctoral dissertation, Princeton University, New Jersey, 1976); and *La Villa Médicis*, 4 vols., ed. A. Chastel and P. Morel (Rome, 1990–91).

23. For the villa see G. Felici, *Villa Ludovisi in Roma* (Rome, 1952), and A. Schiavo, *Villa Ludovisi e Palazzo Margherita* (Rome, 1981).

24. L. Rossini, *Le antichità dei contorni a Roma* (Rome, 1824–26), 256.

25. G. d'Annunzio, *Le vergini delle rocce* (Milan, 1896). For a description of the lost villas of Rome see C. de Seta, *Luoghi e architetture perdute* (Rome and Bari, 1986), and R. Assunto, *Giardini e rimpatrio* (Rome, 1991).

26. For the relationship between the modern villas and the gardens, see M. Fagiolo, "Dagli Horti Sallustiani alle ville barocche tra Pincio e Quirinale," in G. Alessi et al., *I 75 anni dell'I.N.A.* (Rome, 1987), 149–172. See also D. Coffin, *The Villa in the Life of Renaissance Rome*.

27. See M. Fagiolo and M. L. Madonna, "La Roma di Pio IV."

28. For the relationship between Sixtus V's project and the Villa Montalto, see M. Fagiolo, "La Roma di Sisto V: Le matrici del policentrismo," in *Psicon* 8–9 (1976). See also M. L. Madonna, ed., *Roma di Sisto V* (Rome, 1994).

29. For a reconstruction of the history of the Quirinal Gardens, see C. Hülsen, *Römsiches Antikengärten des XVI. Jahrhunderts: Die Villa des Kardinals von Ferrara* (Heidelberg, 1917); G. Briganti, *Il Palazzo del Quirinale* (Rome, 1962); J. Wasserman, "The Quirinal Palace in Rome," in *Art Bulletin* (1963): 205–44; F. Borsi et al., *Il Palazzo del Quirinale* (Rome, 1974); A. Negro, *Guida del Quirinale* (Rome, 1985); and M. Fagiolo, "I giardini papali del vaticano e del Quirinale," in *Giardini regali* (exhibition catalog, Milan, 1998).

30. From an epigram by Michele Silos, *Pinacotheca* (Rome, 1673).

31. D. Fontana, *Della trasportazione dell'Obelisco Vaticano* (Rome, 1590).

32. A. Tagliolini, *Storia del giardino italiano*, 212.

33. Columella, *Libri rei rusticae*, books I, VI, 1 (the treatise is datable ca. 60–65 CE).

34. A. Campitelli, *Villa Borghese* (Rome, 1997), 34. It has been noted that, at first, this area maintains the characteristics of the landscape of Lazio between the Tiber and the northern part of the region: "Narrow valleys formed by the erosion of water, with tufa cliffs that are often sheer. Not rolling hills, therefore, but ravines and vertical drops with roads on the ridges and in the valley bottoms that are difficult to link up. . . . A windy area that was already fertile because it was cultivated *a vigna* (with vineyards); but here this meant not only with vineyards, but with various crops of vegetables and fruit trees." B. di Gaddo, *Villa Borghese. Il giardino e le architetture* (Rome, 1985; 2nd ed., *L'architettura di Villa Borghese*, Rome, 1997).

35. J. Manilli, *Villa Borghese fuori di Porta Pinciana* (Rome, 1650), 161.

36. This term, which originally designated the tent of the military commander, was then applied to the residence in the villa of emperors and other noble owners.

37. See M. Fagiolo, "Le mura e il giardino," in *Il giardino e le mura. Ai confini tra natura e storia*, ed. C. Acidini, G. Galletti, and M. A. Giusti (Florence, 1997), 1–22. I had previously observed that the resemblance of the Villa d'Este at Tivoli to a castrum, with the praetorium and the five *cardines*, should be seen in a wider context in which the orientation of the villa appears to be conditioned by the archaeological grid that characterized the layout of the Roman town itself and of such external elements as the sanctuary of Hercules; see M. *Natura Fagiolo*,

Nartificio (Rome, 1981). With regard to the first boundary wall of the Villa Borghese, it has been observed that the width of the avenues (of two sizes: 9 or 4.5 meters) is comparable to the streets of a regular area of Rome such as the Tridente in Campomarzio; see B. di Gaddo, *L'architettura di Villa Borghese*, 31.

38. See C. H. Heilmann, "Die Entstehungsgeschichte der Villa Borghese," in *Münchner Jahrbuch für Kunstgeschichte* (1973): 116.

39. J. Manilli, *Villa Borghese fuori di Porta Pinciana*, 46.

40. J. Manilli, *Villa Borghese fuori di Porta Pinciana*, 117.

41. This description of Borromini's project is quoted by P. Portoghesi, *Borromini nella cultura europea* (Rome, 1964), 225–26.

42. Regarding the project for flooding the gardens, Portoghesi, *Borromini nella cultura europea*, 262, refers to the similar project, described by Serlio, for the courtyard-*naumachia* of the Villa di Poggioreale in Naples. Moreover, the idea seems to anticipate the festival of the "lake" of Piazza Navona, dating from 1652 and attributed by Maurizio Fagiolo to an idea of Bernini's. The project for the Ark should be related to the Pamphili device of the dove, compared by writers and artists to Noah's dove.

43. C. Benocci, *Villa Doria Pamphili* (Rome, 1996), 188–90.

44. C. Benocci, *Villa Doria Pamphili*, 86.

45. The description by G. Pinarolo (1703) is quoted in C. Benocci, *Villa Doria Pamphili*, 133.

46. For an interpretation of the fountain based on Bellori's description, see C. Benocci, *Villa Doria Pamphili*, 122–32.

47. G. P. Bellori, *Vite de' pittori, scultori et architetti moderni* (Rome, 1672). For the villa see H. Beck and P. C. Bol, eds., *Forschungen zur Villa Albani. Antike Kunst und die Epoche der Aufklärung* (Berlin, 1982), especially the essays by S. Röttgen and E. Schröter; and E. Debenedetti, ed., *Committenze delle famiglia Albani. Note sulla Villa Albani Torlonia* (Rome, 1985), especially the essays by R. Assunto and L. Cassanelli.

48. R. Assunto, *Giardini e rimpatrio* (Rome, 1991), 13.

49. Three letters by Winckelmann, of 1759, 1765, and 1766, respectively (quoted in R. Assunto, *Giardini e rimpatrio*, 14).

50. A statement contained in a contemporary guide to Rome is significant: "I was extremely uncertain as to whether, in my description, I should deal with ancient Rome, or rather with the modern city, since, whatever one may think of the most recent works, the villa is not inferior to any of the most magnificent buildings of antiquity; and this has compelled me to place it at the end of this book, which certainly cannot be concluded in a better way than with an assortment of ancient and modern splendors." R. Venuti, *Roma moderna* (Rome, 1766), 531.

51. L. Cassanelli, "Note per una storia del giardino di Villa Albani," in E. Debenedetti, ed., *Committenze delle famiglia Albani*, 182–83.

52. See M. Bevilacqua, "Nolli e Piranesi a Villa Albani," in *Studi sul Settecento Romano*, ed. E. Debenedetti (Rome, 1993), 71–82.

53. R. Assunto, *Giardini e rimpatrio*, 21, 32.

54. According to an account of 1786, the prince was constructing "a square similar to that of Siena, in which one descends flights of steps, and when it is finished he will hold races of *barberi* [the horses used in the *palio*] in a circus, as happens in the aforementioned city." Quoted by B. di Gaddo, *Villa Borghese*, 157.

55. In addition to the studies on the Villa Borghese mentioned previously, see M. Fagiolo and M. L. Madonna, "Il culto e l'interpretazione dell'antico. Mito, scienza e ideologia," in *Roma dal Neoclassicism al Romanticismo*, ed. F. Borsi (Rome, 1979), 159–239.

56. See M. Fagiolo, "Ideologie di Villa Torlonia. Un mecenate e due architetti nella Roma dell'Ottocento," in *Giuseppe Jappelli e il suo tempo* (Padua, 1981), 549–86; and A. Campitelli, ed., *Villa Torlonia* (Rome, 1997).

57. L. Canina, *Le nuove fabbriche della Villa Borghese denominata Pinciana* (Rome, 1828), 6.

58. G. Checchetelli, *Una giornata di osservazione nel palazzo e nella villa di . . . Alessandro Torlonia* (Rome, 1842), 65–66.

59. L. Canina, *Le nuove fabbriche della Villa Borghese*, 6.

60. L. Canina, *Le nuove fabbriche della Villa Borghese*, 10.

61. L. Canina, *Le nuove fabbriche della Villa Borghese*, 13.

62. L. Canina, *Le nuove fabbriche della Villa Borghese*, 9.

63. L. Canina, *Le nuove fabbriche della Villa Borghese*, 14.

64. G. Checchetelli, *Una giornata di osservazione*.

65. G. Checchetelli, *Una giornata di osservazione*.

66. G. Checchetelli, *Una giornata di osservazione*.

67. G. Checchetelli, *Una giornata di osservazione*.

68. G. Checchetelli, *Una giornata di osservazione*.

69. G. Checchetelli, *Una giornata di osservazione*.

70. G. Checchetelli, *Una giornata di osservazione*.

71. G. Checchetelli, *Una giornata di osservazione*.

72. G. Checchetelli, *Una giornata di osservazione*.

73. G. Checchetelli, *Una giornata di osservazione*

The term *Palatium*, which in antiquity designated the imperial palace, derives from the Latin name of the hill, Mons Palatinus. From the outset, the Roman emperors built their residences on the Palatine because it was the site of the mythical foundation of Rome by Romulus. First Caesar's adopted son Octavius settled on the hill in a house connected directly to the temple of Apollo, the sun god believed to have protected him in his rise to power as the emperor Augustus. The first great imperial residence, the Domus Tiberiana built by Tiberius (14–37 CE), is now largely buried beneath the sixteenth-century Farnese Gardens. But Domitian was responsible for the real *Palatium* or Domus Augustana (that is, house of caesars or emperors), designed by his architect Rabirius (ca. 81–92 CE).

The complex comprised two nuclei: the Domus Flavia—the state apartments—and the residential Domus Augustana. In the first nucleus, a peristyle surrounded a vast octagonal fountain in the form of a labyrinth; there was an oval fountain near the Cenatio Iovis, the imposing apsed dining room. Other important water features have been identified in the Domus Augustana: "In the center of a large peristyle an ornamental pool is visible. A *tempietto* rose on a high podium forming an island in

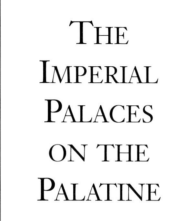

THE IMPERIAL PALACES ON THE PALATINE

the pool; this was reached by a small bridge. We know that, in the Flavian palace, there was a temple of Minerva, a goddess particularly venerated by the emperor: it is quite possible this stood in the center of the basin" (F. Coarelli, 1974). A fountain comprising four curved elements—*peltae*, the shields of the mythical Amazons—facing each other lay at the center of another large courtyard; in the middle of the same courtyard there was a hall flanked by two *nymphaea*.

Of particular importance is the Domitian-era stadium or circus, which extended for about 150 meters along the eastern edge of the complex. This is evidently the Hippodromus Palatii mentioned by early Christian sources, and probably constitutes the prototype of the garden-hippodrome, which later became a common feature of the gardens of emperors and wealthy patrons such as Pliny the Younger. The curved side toward the valley of the Circus of Maxentius and the remains of the spina are linked to the typology of the circus; in the center of the long external side are the remains of a semicircular tribune. Later, in the fifth century, perhaps during Theodoric's reign, a smaller oval enclosure in the form of the arena of an amphitheater was inserted in the interior of the circus.

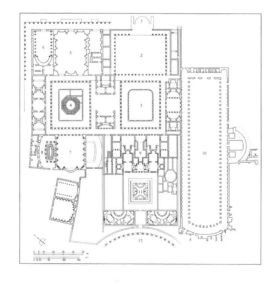

Left: Plan of the imperial palaces on the Palatine Hill (from H. Stierlin, 1984). On the left is the Domus Flavia, in the center the Domus Augustana, on the right the stadium.

Right: Ruins of the imperial palaces.

Ruins of the imperial palaces.

View with the casino of the Belvedere of the Farnese Gardens.

RUINS OF THE IMPERIAL PALACES.

RUINS OF THE IMPERIAL PALACES.

FOUNTAIN IN THE COURTYARD OF THE DOMUS AUGUSTANA WITH MOTIFS IN THE
FORM OF *PELTAE*, THE SHIELDS OF THE MYTHICAL AMAZONS.

LOGGIA OF THE BELVEDERE IN THE FARNESE GARDENS.

Overleaf:
Cryptoporticus from the Neronian period (it linked various parts of the imperial palaces). Remains of mosaic pavements and stuccoes remain on the ceilings, with Cupids amid plant motifs.

DETAIL OF A PATH IN THE GARDENS LEADING TOWARD THE FARNESE GARDENS.

RIGHT: THE FIGURE OF A HARPY, DETAIL OF A DECORATIVE BAS-RELIEF.

Overleaf: Stadium or hippodrome (built by Domitian, and then modified under Hadrian and Septimius Severus). The imposing imperial tribune was built on a circular plan.

VILLA CHIGI FARNESINA

Between 1505 and 1512, the Sienese banker and patron of the arts Agostino Chigi, one of the great protagonists of the economic and cultural life of papal Rome, built his suburban residence. Designed by the Sienese architect and painter Baldassare Peruzzi, the facade of the main building, on two floors, is composed of a five-arched loggia (Loggia di Psiche) between two projecting wings; the one facing the Tiber also originally had an open loggia (Loggia di Galatea). The walls are divided by pilasters and crowned by a deep frieze with stucco putti and festoons inspired by the bas-reliefs of the Pantheon (between them are the small attic windows). At the rear there was formerly a quadrangular *giardino segreto* (walled garden). The whole building, with its simple, rationally linked architectural forms, clearly of classical inspiration, was, as Vasari wrote, "created with the sense of grace that may be seen today, not built but truly born." Light from the garden penetrated through the many openings and was reflected on the facades, with their sgraffito decorations featuring plant and mythological motifs.

That the villa was a meeting-place for the cultured and a locus of refined leisure may be dimly imagined in the park surrounding it and separating it from the rest of the city; unfortunately, nothing is known about the old gardens. The contemporary text by Blosio Palladio, drawing on the myth of the gardens of the Hesperides, mentions the genera of plants (roses, violets, lilies, lemons, laurels, myrtles, cypresses), the lawns, the walks often covered with roofs of woven reeds, and the *boschetti* (small wooded areas); part of the area was planted with vines and fruit trees. The stables designed by Raphael were located on Via Lungara; by the Tiber there was a portico with a fishpond underneath, also

attributed to Raphael. This was the scene of sumptuous banquets and cultured gatherings: "Inside the voices of Apollo and the nine joyful Muses resound eternally," Gallo wrote in 1511. Both the stables and the portico on the Tiber were short-lived: of the former, only a fragment of the external wall with coupled pilasters remains; the latter was damaged a number of times when the river flooded. Eventually it was abandoned; it had already completely disappeared by the mid-sixteenth century.

The magnificence of the architecture and gardens is matched by the splendor of the decoration of the interior of the villa, where the humanistic theme of the journey of the soul through difficulties to reach love is treated. Around 1511, Raphael, who had become the favorite artist and confidant of Agostino Chigi, painted *Galatea* in the loggia. On the ceiling is a complex composition of mythological scenes that, seen in an astrological light, illustrate the auspicious horoscope of Chigi, who was born at midnight on November 29, 1466 (F. Saxl, 1934; M. Quinlan, 1984). By the end of 1517, on the vault of the entrance loggia, Raphael and his pupils had painted the episodes of the story of Cupid and Psyche deriving from Ovid.

The decorations of a more private character on the upper floor comprise the huge Sala delle Prospettive by Peruzzi and, in what was the bedroom of Agostino Chigi (whose wedding took place in the villa in the presence of the pope), the *Marriage of Alexander and Roxane* by Sodoma.

Soon after Chigi's death, in 1520, the building and gardens were abandoned; the property was purchased by the cardinal Alessandro Farnese in 1579 and, when his family died out in the eighteenth century, it went to the Bourbons of Naples.

Plan du Palais.

Left: Plan of the Villa Chigi Farnesina (engraving from Letarouilly, 1857).

Right: Water god (ancient mascaron reused in a fountain).

THE VILLA FROM VIA DELLA LUNGARA. ON THE RIGHT IS THE *GIARDINO SEGRETO*.

PUTTI BEARING FESTOONS OF FRUIT AND FLOWERS, FROM WHICH PASTORAL
SYRINXES HANG, ON THE FRIEZE.

Overleaf: Loggia di
Galatea. On the left is the
fresco by Raphael for
which the loggia is
named; the lunettes con-
taining mythological
scenes were frescoed by
Sebastiano da Piombo,
while the landscapes were
painted in the seventeenth
century, after the arches
had been filled in.

Agostino Chigi's horoscope (fresco by Baldassare Peruzzi) on ceiling of the Loggia di Galatea. In the center are two panels depicting the myth of Perseus and Medusa, and the nymph Callisto.

Right: Detail of a candelabrum in the Loggia di Galatea (fresco attributed to Domenico Beccafumi).

DETAILS OF THE CEILING OF THE LOGGIA DI GALATEA (FRESCOES BY BALDASSARE PERUZZI).
ABOVE LEFT: GANYMEDE AND THE EAGLE (AQUARIUS); BELOW LEFT: APOLLO
AND THE CENTAUR (SAGITTARIUS); ABOVE RIGHT: DIANA AND ERIGONE (VIRGO);
BELOW RIGHT: HERCULES AND THE HYDRA OF LERNA (CANCER).

Overleaf: Detail of the Loggia di Galatea (fresco by Raphael). Galatea rides a shell-chariot.

LEFT: DETAIL OF THE CEILING OF THE LOGGIA DI GALATEA
(FRESCO BY BALDASSARE PERUZZI) SHOWING VENUS WITH THE GOAT (CAPRICORN).

Detail of the Loggia di Galatea (fresco by Raphael) with Cupid and dolphins.

Right: Detail of the Loggia di Galatea (fresco by Sebastiano del Piombo)
with the figure of Polyphemus.

DETAIL OF *THE FALL OF PERDIX*. PERDIX WAS PUSHED BY HIS UNCLE, DAEDALUS.

Lunette in the Loggia di Galatea with a colossal head
attributed to Baldassare Peruzzi.

LOGGIA DI PSICHE (FRESCOES BY RAPHAEL AND ASSISTANTS).

Ceiling of the Loggia di Psiche (frescoes by Raphael and assistants).
In the center are *Council of the Gods* and *Banquet of the Gods*.

Overleaf: Detail of a spandrel on the ceiling of the Loggia di Psiche (frescoes by Raphael and assistants), showing *Cupid and the Three Graces.*

Second overleaf: Sala delle Prospettive (frescoes by Baldassare Peruzzi and assistants; the frieze with mythological scenes has also been attributed to Giulio Romano).

SALA DELLE PROSPETTIVE (FRESCO BY AN ARTIST IN THE CIRCLE OF
BALDASSARE PERUZZI) WITH *VULCAN'S FORGE* ON THE CHIMNEYPIECE.

DETAILS OF THE SALA DELLE PROSPETTIVE
(FRESCOES BY ARTISTS IN THE CIRCLE OF BALDASSARE PERUZZI)
WITH *THE CHARIOT OF AURORA* AND *VENUS GRIEVING OVER ADONIS'S BODY*.

Overleaf: Detail of the Sala delle Prospettive with *Deucalion and Pyrrha* (fresco by an artist in the circle of Baldassare Peruzzi). The two progenitors, the only survivors of the great flood in Greek mythology, throw stones over their shoulders, and these are then transformed into men and women.

ALESSANDRO CHIGI'S BEDROOM (FRESCOES BY SODOMA). ABOVE LEFT: ROXANE;
BELOW LEFT: *THE FAMILY OF DARIUS BEFORE ALEXANDER*;
ABOVE RIGHT: *THE BATTLE OF ISSUS*; BELOW RIGHT: TWO BYSTANDERS.

LEFT: ALESSANDRO CHIGI'S BEDROOM (FRESCOES BY SODOMA) WITH
THE MARRIAGE OF ALEXANDER AND ROXANE.

Overleaf: Alessandro
Chigi's bedroom (frescoes
by Sodoma). Left:
*Alexander on His Horse
Bucephalus in the Battle of
Issus.* Right: *The Marriage
of Alexander and Roxane.*

Sited near the Ponte Milvio, on the slopes of Monte Mario, the villa was built from 1517 onward to designs by Raphael for Cardinal Giulio de' Medici (who became pope in 1523 as Clement VII). Antonio da Sangallo the Younger was also involved in the scheme, as was Giulio Romano subsequently. The overall project constituted a dream that was only partially realized—after being brutally interrupted by the sack of Rome in 1527—to globally revive the villas of the ancients: "[Raphael] enlarged the rooms flanking the loggia, and arranged them (as in the Villa Medici at Poggio a Caino) for palace life, so that the cardinal's court could stay there for long periods at a time. It seems that the cardinal preferred to spend his longer sojourns in the suburban area beyond the Ponte Milvio (Milvian Bridge) rather than live in the crush of the city center. Here his mania for building was unrestricted, and only here could he achieve in total liberty his ideal of a suburban villa in the antique style with loggias, a hippodrome, theater, *nymphaeum*, *peschiere*, and ample terraced gardens—all elements that Alberti had envisaged and whose prototype was the villa of Giulio de' Medici's ancestors at Fiesole. . . . The cardinal and his friends would have been able to take the baths in real thermae, perform dramatic works in the Vitruvian theater, organize horse races in the hippodrome, and entertain in real cenationes" (C. L. Frommel, 1994).

The overall project may be reconstructed thanks to both a series of drawings and a letter by Raphael (possibly written in 1519 with the advice of the humanist Fabio Calvo and addressed to Count Baldassare Castiglione), which is clearly influenced by Vitruvius's treatise on architecture and the famous letters by Pliny

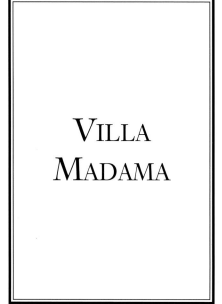

VILLA MADAMA

the Younger describing his villas at Tifernum and Laurentium.

Although only half of the circular courtyard was built and the theater and hippodrome were never realized, what remains of the villa gives us at least a partial idea of the splendor and high qualitative level of Raphael's "antiquarian" dream. It is sufficient to mention the spectacular loggia, decorated after Raphael's death in 1520 by Giulio Romano and Giovanni da Udine. "Stuccoes, grotesques, decorations, niches, shells, a dome and two groin vaults, barrel vaults, panels: the interior has a continuous flow, an interchange between space, sculpture, fictive perspective, pictorial illusionism, and the overall structure. And the same dynamic interchange of views and perceptions involves the natural scene, the landscape" (S. Ray, 1974).

The *xystus*, the open space or hanging garden in front of the loggia (note in particular the small *nymphaeum all'antica* with the Elephant Fountain by Giovanni da Udine), led through a portal flanked by two colossal statues by Baccio Bandinelli to the next garden, laid out on a long terrace and crossed by paths lined with pots and antique sculptures. Under the *xystus* lies the fishpond with the arched substructures recalling the archetype of the Ponte Milvio.

On the death of Clement VII in 1534 the villa passed successively to Cardinal Ippolito and Alessandro de' Medici, the duke of Florence, and then to the latter's widow, "Madama Reale," Margaret of Austria, the natural daughter of the emperor Charles V and then the wife of the duke of Parma, Ottavio Farnese. The villa was frequently used for official receptions for illustrious guests visiting Rome, and today it is still used by the Italian Foreign Ministry for similar purposes.

VILLA MADAMA

Left: Plan (from Percier and Fontaine, 1824). From the bottom: the semicircular courtyard (2), the loggia (4), the hanging garden with the Elephant Fountain (8, 9), and the fishpond (7). At the top is the gateway leading to the terraced garden.

Right: Elephant Fountain (attributed to Giovanni da Udine). The sculpture commemorates the famous elephant Annone, brought to Rome by a diplomatic mission from Goa as a gift from King Manuel I of Portugal to Leo X.

Overleaf: Hanging garden seen from the loggia. In the background are the *Giants* by Baccio Bandinelli.

DETAIL OF ONE OF THE *GIANTS* BY BACCIO BANDINELLI.

RIGHT: TERRACED GARDEN.

Overleaf: The incomplete exedra of the semicircular courtyard (part of the unfinished circular courtyard).

Second overleaf: Loggia. The vaults, pilasters, and exedra are decorated with stuccoes by Giovanni da Udine and frescoes by Giulio Romano.

CENTRAL VAULT OF THE LOGGIA (MYTHOLOGICAL FIGURES, ALLEGORIES OF THE
SEASONS, AND MEDICI EMBLEMS).

Coat of arms of Leo X in the central vault of the loggia.

EASTERN VAULT OF THE LOGGIA (FRESCOES BY GIULIO ROMANO AND STUCCOES BY GIOVANNI DA UDINE). IN THE CENTRAL MEDALLION IS GALATEA ON HER SHELL-CHARIOT.

EASTERN VAULT OF THE LOGGIA (FRESCOES BY GIULIO ROMANO AND STUCCOES BY
GIOVANNI DA UDINE).

Western vault of the loggia (frescoes by Giulio Romano and stuccoes by
Giovanni da Udine).

WESTERN VAULT OF THE LOGGIA (FRESCOES BY GIULIO ROMANO AND STUCCOES BY
GIOVANNI DA UDINE). IN THE CENTRAL MEDALLION IS NEPTUNE ON HIS CHARIOT.

Baldassarre Turini da Pescia, a senior official of the Curia under two Medici popes (he was datary of Leo X and *cameriere segreto* [dignitary of the papal court] of Clement VIII), commissioned Giulio Romano to design his villa, which was built around 1524–1527. At that time the whole area was located outside the city walls, and the casino was used only during the summer months. According to tradition, the villa is located on the site of Martial's villa; the plaque in the loggia bearing a quotation from the poet, "Hinc totam licet aestimare Romam" (From here you can appraise the whole of Rome), stresses the identification of the new villa with the ancient one and reveals the humanistic design to revive every aspect of the character and spirit of antiquity.

The open loggia on the crest of the hill, looking out over the whole city, constitutes the most outstanding feature of the building. Soaring gracefully in the landscape, the elegant Serlian loggia occupies a large part of the rear facade overlooking the valley. On the sides and main facade, the refined architectural design of the piano nobile, embellished with a row of coupled pilasters in white stucco, is drawn or engraved on the surface of the walls, a reinterpretation of the bas-reliefs of antiquity.

After the sack of Rome in 1527, the interior decoration of the villa was executed. Initially it was carried out under the supervision of Giulio Romano and was concluded before the end of 1531, probably with the participation of Giovanni da Udine (the

VILLA LANTE ON THE JANICULUM

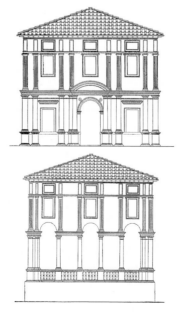

stuccoes on the ceiling of the loggia), Polidoro da Caravaggio, and Benedetto Pagni da Pescia.

In "The Life of Giulio Romano, Painter" in his *Lives of the Artists*, Vasari praised the artist for "having himself painted there a number of stories of Numa Pompilius, whose tomb was located on that site. In the stufa he painted a number of stories of Venus and Cupid, and of Apollo and Hyacinthus, with the aid of his assistants." Although most of the decoration has now been lost or removed, some of the rooms have ceilings decorated with stuccoes and frescoes with grotesques. The decoration of a room on the piano nobile is particularly original; here there are four tondos with copies of female faces by Raphael, a tribute to the great artist on the part of Turini, who was his friend, confidant, and executor. In the salon, within a complex stucco frame containing the coats of arms and *imprese* of the Turini and Clement VII (later modified by the Lante, the new owners of the villa from the mid-sixteenth century onward) and the busts of Numa Pompilius, Cloelia, Bacchus and Janus, were frescoes depicting the stories of Numa Pompilius (now in the Palazzo Zuccari, Rome), deriving from Livy and chosen because of the close topographic link with the Janiculum. In the background of the panel of the *Discovery on the Janiculum of Numa Pompilius's Sarcophagus* is depicted the facade of the villa, with part of the surrounding gardens laid out in parterres around the avenues giving access to the main entrance.

INTERIOR OF THE LOGGIA.

CEILING OF THE LOGGIA. THE STUCCO DECORATION, ATTRIBUTED TO
GIOVANNI DA UDINE, IS DATED 1531.

CEILING OF THE MAIN SALON ON THE PIANO NOBILE. IN THE CENTER IS THE COAT
OF ARMS OF THE BORGHESE POPE, PAUL V. THE PANELS FORMERLY CONTAINED THE
FRESCOES DEPICTING THE STORIES OF NUMA POMPILIUS NOW IN THE PALAZZO
ZUCCARI, ROME (BIBLIOTECA HERTZIANA).

Ceiling of the main salon on the piano nobile. Busts portraying Numa
Pompilius, Bacchus, Janus, Cloelia (stuccoes ca. 1530–40).

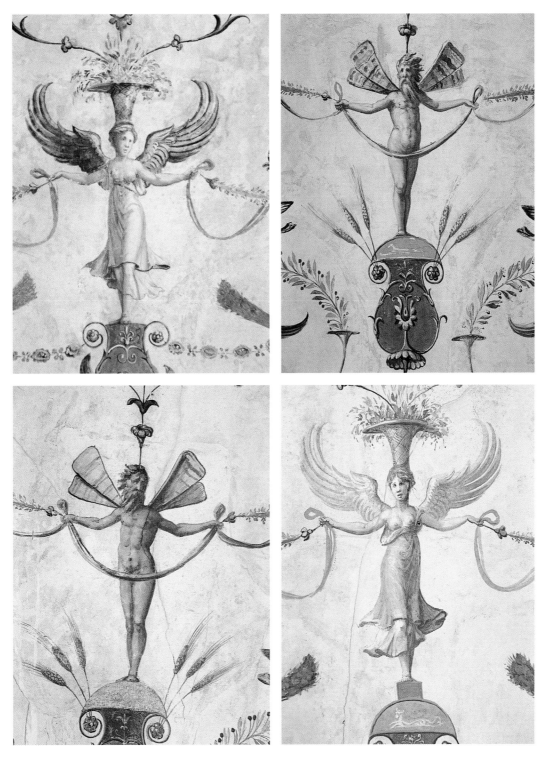

DETAILS OF FRESCOES DEPICTING GROTESQUES.

LEFT: CEILING OF THE "ROOM OF THE WOMEN LOVED BY RAPHAEL."

DETAILS OF THE FRESCOES DEPICTING FOUR FEMALE PORTRAITS BY RAPHAEL ON
THE CEILING OF THE "ROOM OF THE WOMEN LOVED BY RAPHAEL."
(THE MELPOMENE MUSE FROM THE *PARNASSUS* IN THE STANZA DELLA SEGNATURE,
THE *FORNARINA*, AND THE *DONNA VELATA* ARE IDENTIFIABLE.)

CEILING OF THE "ROOM OF THE WOMEN LOVED BY RAPHAEL." IN THE CENTER IS
THE SEVENTEENTH-CENTURY COAT OF ARMS OF CARDINAL MARCELLO LANTE.

As soon as he was elected pope, Julius III (originally Giovanni Maria de' Ciocchi del Monte, pope 1550–55) decided to build a splendid villa on his land on the Via Flaminia, commissioning three important architects to design it: Giacomo da Vignola, Bartolomeo Ammannati, and Giorgio Vasari, under the direction of Michelangelo. In his desire for imperial and antiquarian magnificence it is likely that the pope intended to link himself, through the name of the villa, to both Julius II, the patron of the Belvedere Court, and Cardinal Giulio de' Medici, who commissioned the Villa Madama, evidently a model for the new villa.

We do not know whether Julius III intended to create a sort of suburban Domus Aurea (Nero's palace was an obligatory prototype of the villas and palaces of the sixteenth century), but in any case, as a tribute to the pope's name, the Villa del Monte had to embrace the *monti* (hills) of Rome, both within and without the city. (In the salon on the piano nobile, the famous seven hills of Rome were depicted next to a representation of the villa.)

The house, with its rear facade consisting of a semicircular colonnade, can certainly be attributed to Vignola, Ammannati designed the central loggia in the form of a *scenae frons*, while Vasari was perhaps responsible for the arrangement on different levels. The spectacular enfilade of spaces, with the transparent "partitions" created by the vestibules, porticos, and loggias, may have been Michelangelo's idea.

The true heart of the villa is the fountain of the Caryatids, which is, in effect, an underground fountain of the Acqua Vergine (the inscription on a medal of 1552 seems to identify the villa with the fountain: "Fons Virginis Villae Iuliae"). The *nymphaeum* is con-

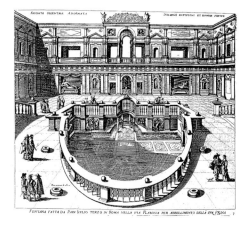

structed with a complex system of external and internal staircases linking three different levels, leading down to the deep spring of water, which, in a sense, becomes the focus of the perspective of the whole composition, to use an expression of Ammannati himself: "the splendid Acqua Vergine . . . this being the principal point from where everything may be seen; and one might well say that this is the center of perspective."

Some years later, the French scholar Jean-Jacques Boissard described the sumptuousness of the villa with its magnificent display of works of art, of which very little remains: "Everything is made of precious marble: the building is supported by columns of Parian and green marble. . . . The floor is made of chalcedony, alabaster, porphyry, ophite, and simetite. . . . From the grottoes, with their skillfully constructed vaults, a large quantity of limpid water gushes forth. . . . There are naked putti sitting on dolphins. Here and there are disposed Naiads and leaping satyrs. There are statues of Bacchus, Apollo, Diana, Pallas, Hebe, Hercules, Vesta, Venus, Mars, Antinous, Mercury, Vertumnus, naked shepherds, Curetes, Maenads and countless other ancient figures, without including the splendid inscriptions and precious marble with which the walls are encrusted."

The villa could be designated both a theater and a museum: "All the elements of the villa serve to frame hundreds of ancient statues. Thus the architectural complex assumes the appearance of a huge antiquarium, a building type that is often underestimated" (C. Davis, 1976). This is obviously a living concept of the museum, not only as a place of veneration (the "seat of the Muses") but of a dialectic encounter with the ancient world, in line with the antiquarianism then in vogue in the court of the popes and cardinals.

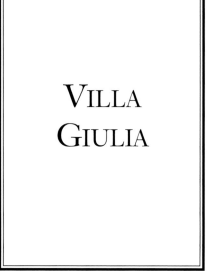

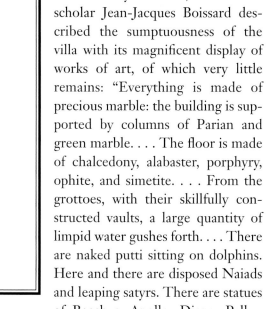

VILLA
GIULIA

Left: Second courtyard with Ammannati's *nymphaeum* (engraving by A. Lafréry, 1550).

Right: Detail of a caryatid in the *nymphaeum* (sculpture by Bartolomeo Ammannati).

Overleaf: Rear facade of the villa consisting of a semicircular colonnade, seen from the opening of the loggia-theater (formerly decorated with *sgraffito*, stuccoes, and ancient statues).

Second overleaf: The semicircular colonnade-ambulatory at the rear facade of the villa (designed by Giacomo da Vignola).

DETAIL OF THE DECORATION OF THE SEMICIRCULAR COLONNADE-AMBULATORY.

CUPIDS FROLICKING IN PERGOLAS OF VINES AND ROSES (FRESCOES ATTRIBUTED TO
PIETRO VENALE DA IMOLA).

LEFT AND ABOVE: DETAILS OF THE DECORATION OF THE SEMICIRCULAR
COLONNADE-AMBULATORY (FRESCOES ATTRIBUTED TO PIETRO VENALE DA IMOLA),
SHOWING CUPIDS FROLICKING AND BIRDS IN PERGOLAS OF ROSES AND VINES.

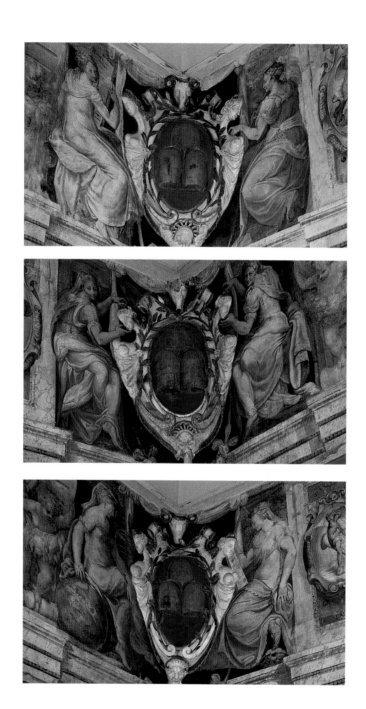

ROOM OF THE SEVEN HILLS (FRESCOES ATTRIBUTED TO TADDEO ZUCCARI AND
PROSPERO FONTANA). ON THE FRIEZE ARE STUCCO HERALDIC DEVICES
OF JULIUS III BETWEEN ALLEGORICAL FIGURES.

ROOM OF THE SEVEN HILLS (FRESCO ATTRIBUTED TO TADDEO ZUCCARI AND
PROSPERO FONTANA). THE FRIEZE SHOWS THE VILLA AND THE FOUNTAIN
ON THE VIA FLAMINIA.

Overleaf: First courtyard from the semicircular colonnade.

Second overleaf: Side of first courtyard. Ancient statues were placed in the niches in the side walls; in the upper row, ovals with portraits of the Caesars.

Above and right: Loggia between the first courtyard and the *Nymphaeum*.
The stuccoes feature mythological figures in the side panels.

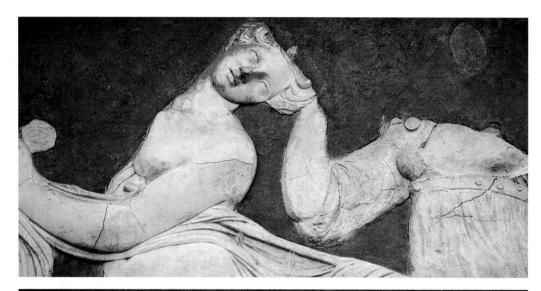

ABOVE AND LEFT: LOGGIA BETWEEN THE FIRST COURTYARD AND THE *NYMPHAEUM*.
THE STUCCOES FEATURE MYTHOLOGICAL FIGURES IN THE SIDE PANELS.

Overleaf:
Nymphaeum. Ammannati's fountain is visible below. The *peperino* statues at the sides of the river-gods Tiber and Arno (1554) are among the few surviving elements of the magnificent original decoration.

THE *NYMPHAEUM* WITH THE FOUR CARYATIDS SCULPTED BY AMMANNATI.

LEFT: DETAIL OF A CARYATID IN BAS-RELIEF NEXT TO A SIDE DOOR.

Head of the statue of Arno.

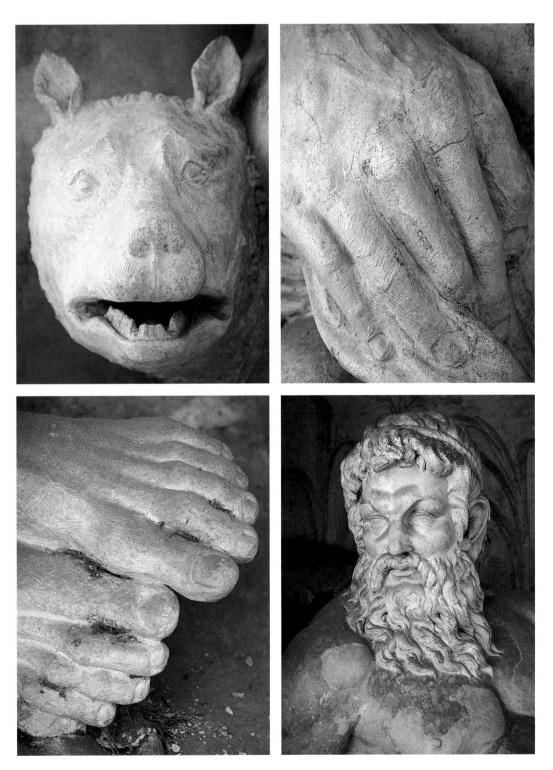

DETAILS OF THE STATUE OF TIBER.

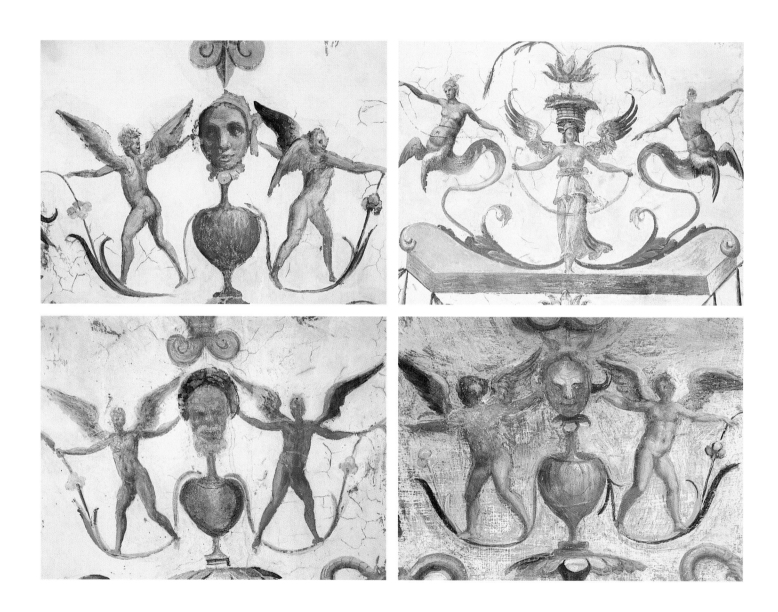

ABOVE AND RIGHT: DETAILS OF THE CEILING OF THE GROTTO OF THE *NYMPHAEUM*
(FRESCOES ATTRIBUTED TO TADDEO ZUCCARI). THE DECORATIVE CYCLE COMPRISES
MYTHOLOGICAL FIGURES, THE FOUR SEASONS, AND TWO SOLAR CHARIOTS.

During the sixteenth century, the Vatican Gardens were created in three parts: the Belvedere Court, Paul III's walled garden, and the Casino of Pius IV. The latter was initiated by Paul IV (originally Gian Pietro Carafa, pope 1555–59) in 1558 as a retreat allowing respite from the excessive worldliness of the Vatican palaces. The architect and antiquarian Pirro Ligorio continued the building for Pius IV (originally Giovanni Angelo de' Medici, pope 1559–65), with a new program comprising two small *tempietti*, a small building crowned by a pediment with a loggia, and the casino itself on two stories (it now houses the Papal Academy of the Sciences). The four buildings are linked by an oval court containing a central fountain, which may be associated with models of the ancient *naumachiae*.

The small complex constitutes a remarkable concentration of forms and symbols: it is crowded with images that are both fascinating and evocative, with particular prominence being given to the themes of water and theater. The pontificate of Pius IV immediately appeared to be surrounded by an aura of peace, welfare, and public happiness, in a climate influenced by classical culture. The Aurora on the pediment of the loggia marked the beginning of a new age, as did the bas-relief depicting Amalthea, alluding to both the mythical golden age and the zodiacal sign of Capricorn that was common to the empire of Augustus, the duchy of Cosimo de' Medici, and Pius IV's pontificate (which began under this sign). The key figure for the interpretation of the functional character and the iconological program of the casino may be found in the central

CASINO OF POPE PIUS IV IN VATICAN CITY

panel of the loggia: Pierus, the mountain in Thessaly where Zeus coupled with Mnemosyne. In an Ionic temple, flanked by trees on the top of a mountain, "Pierius" (as the name is spelled in the inscription), an effeminate figure holds a mask in his right hand; with his left hand, he leans on an amphora from which water gushes. Five elements that are combined in the overall meaning and the formal and functional character of the villa clearly emerge: myth, religion (the *tempietto*), nature (the tree-clad mountain, qualifying the site as a "sacred grove" and "sacred mountain"), water (the amphora), and theater (the comic mask). To these themes are added those evoked by numerous other stucco bas-reliefs encrusting the walls of both the casino and the loggia. The Muses flanking Pierius appear to be linked not only to the arts, music, and theater, but also to banquets, water, time, the myth of the golden age, and the allegory of memory.

While the loggia, below which is a fishpond, was certainly intended to serve as a dining room (resembling the Roman *cenatio*), the casino itself—decorated on the exterior with mythological scenes and inside with frescoes depicting mainly religious subjects—initially probably housed the learned meetings of the Academy of the Noctes Vaticanae under the direction of the erudite and very young cardinal nephew, Carlo Borromeo. During the pontificate of Pius V (1566–72), a radial botanical garden was laid out by Michele Mercati below the casino, toward the Belvedere Court (it was later moved elsewhere). The same pope stripped the casino of a large number of its ancient sculptures.

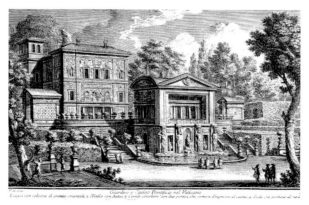

Giardino e Casino Pontificio nel Vaticano

Left: Casino of Pius IV (engraving by G. Vasi, 1761). In the foreground is the loggia with the original arrangement of telamones in the form of satyrs.

Right: Detail of Pius IV's coat of arms on the facade.

Overleaf: Facade of the loggia facing the Belvedere Court (designed by Pirro Ligorio). The lower tier, with a statue of Cybele in the center, was originally divided by four colossal statues of satyrs, replaced at the beginning of the twentieth century by pilasters decorated with mosaics.

Second overleaf: A *tempietto* and the facade of the casino (designed by Pirro Ligorio).

Third overleaf: Oval courtyard with the casino, one of the two *tempietti*, and the loggia (designed by Pirro Ligorio).

Fourth overleaf: Loggia (designed by Pirro Ligorio).

DETAIL OF THE CEILING OF THE LOGGIA (FRESCOES BY FEDERICO ZUCCARI) WITH
MOSES, VENUS, AND ADONIS, AND STUCCO BAS-RELIEFS IN ANTIQUE STYLE.

RIGHT: DETAIL OF THE CEILING OF THE LOGGIA (FRESCOES BY FEDERICO
ZUCCARI) WITH VENUS AND TRITONS.

PUTTO ON A DOLPHIN IN THE FOUNTAIN IN THE CENTER OF THE COURTYARD
(SCULPTURE BY JACOPO DA CASIGNOLA).

LEFT: THE CASINO SEEN FROM THE LOGGIA (DESIGNED BY PIRRO LIGORIO).

Overleaf: Entrance hall of the casino (designed by Pirro Ligorio). In the semidome of the exedra are frescoes and stuccoes depicting stories of Moses. On the wall to the right is a bas-relief portraying Diana of the Ephesians.

Detail of one of the two exedrae in the entrance hall.

Ceiling of the entrance hall (frescoes by Federico Zuccari and assistants).

ENTRANCE HALL OF THE CASINO. THE FRIEZE INCLUDES CIRCENSIAN SCENES
(FRESCOES BY ARTISTS IN THE CIRCLE OF FEDERICO ZUCCARI).

RIGHT: GROTESQUE MASCARON IN THE ENTRANCE HALL (MOSAIC OF PEBBLES AND SHELLS).

Details of frescoes and grotesques in the exedrae in the entrance hall.

Left: Detail of *Diana of the Ephesians* in the entrance hall (bas-relief in
various materials).

During the sixteenth century the Vatican Gardens were, above all, "gardens of stone," containing only a few fountains. An important turning point was around 1610, when Paul V (originally Camillo Borghese, pope 1605–21) ordered the new Acqua Paola to be linked to the Vatican Hill. The idea of revitalizing the Belvedere Court was debated "with fountains, perspectives, and other beautiful things" (as an *avviso di Roma*, a sort of journalistic account, stated in 1609). The proposed revisions would have involved the destruction of the Sistine Library and the construction of *nymphaea*, cascades, and ornamental fountains. In the end, all that was done was to move the pine-cone fountain from the demolished quadriporticus of Old St. Peter's to the gigantic niche of the Belvedere Court, while the old fountain was rebuilt in the Piazza of St. Peter's surmounted by a scaly dome imitating the appearance of the pine cone.

The new water supply fed many important fountains constructed by Paul V's architects, Carlo Maderno, Giovanni Vasanzio, and Martino Ferrabosco. Particularly unusual is the Fontana dei Torri or del Sacramento. Named for its circular display of jets of water recalling the shape of a monstrance, the fountain transforms the defensive structures of an internal wall of the Vatican into a display of water; the central cascade confirms the "fortitude" of the water and the heraldic dragons of the Borghese family. Even more remarkable is the Fontana della Galera, built in 1620–21 at the foot of the Belvedere Court, next to an artificial cliff dating from Julius III's pontificate (rebuilt at the end

FOUNTAINS OF VATICAN CITY

of the eighteenth century). It consisted of "a huge ship made of metal (copper and lead), built with every detail of the sails, decks, and even of the gun ports from which water can spout forcefully" (C. d'Onofrio, 1986). Aside from the jest of the cannons that spew forth water rather than shot, this model seems to represent the concept of the bold voyage of the "bark" of the Church, now transformed into an invincible galleon.

But it is above all the Fontana dello Scoglio or dell'Aquilone that constitutes a natural answer to the Fontanone del Gianicolo, the most important fountain of the Acqua Paola in Rome. The oval *nymphaeum* forms a sort of rustic fountain, well suited to the *bosco* (wooded area) of the Belvedere. The theater of rocks is dominated by the Borghese emblems (an eagle above and dragons in two caves) alternating with Tritons on dolphins. The water spurts out in jets or falls in rainlike sprays and cascades; particularly notable is the idea of the small cascade that, channeled between rocky borders, forms the edge of the pool.

The Fontana degli Specchi and other fountains since demolished date from Paul V's pontificate. In the following centuries the attention of the popes tended to focus on the *giardino segreto*, which was extended and redesigned with the name *giardino quadrato* (square garden), and the modernization of the bosco as an English garden of lawns, statues, cippi, and a number of new fountains—for instance, the nineteenth-century Fontana del Globo (with the coat of arms of Gregory XVI, now reused in a more modern fountain).

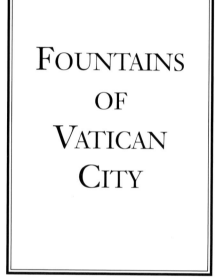

FONTANA DETTA LO SCOGLIO NEL GIARDINO DI BELVEDERE NEL PALAZZO PONTIFICIO
di Vaticano Architettura di Carlo Maderni

Triton on a Dolphin (sculpture by Stefano Maderno) in the
Fontana dell'Aquilone (designed by Carlo Maderno, Giovanni Vasanzio
and Martino Ferrabosco, 1611–12).

Left: Statue of Nereid in the Fontana dell'Aquilone (designed by
Carlo Maderno, Giovanni Vasanzio, and Martino Ferrabosco, 1611–12).

DETAIL OF THE HERALDIC DRAGON OF THE BORGHESE POPE, PAUL V,
IN THE FONTANA DELL'AQUILONE.

Italian garden with topiaries.

PARTERRE IN THE FRENCH STYLE.

RIGHT: DETAIL OF A FOUNTAIN.

ABOVE: THE FONTANA DELLA GALERA WITH THE ARTIFICIAL CLIFF AND THE
FACADE EXECUTED IN 1779, DURING THE PONTIFICATE OF PIUS VI.

LEFT: DETAIL OF THE GALLEON IN COPPER AND LEAD (1620–21)
IN THE FONTANA DELLA GALERA.

FOUNTAIN WITH A YOUNG TRITON IN THE ROSE GARDEN.

FOUNTAIN WITH A YOUNG TRITON IN THE ROSE GARDEN.

The Villa Medici is located on the site of the gardens of Lucullus (*horti Luculliani*), which later belonged to the Acilii and the Pincii. In 1564 Cardinal Giovanni Ricci (1495–1574), after buying a vineyard near the Aurelian walls from the Crescenzi, began to build the villa (designed by Nanni di Baccio Bigio) and lay out the gardens, in which ancient statues and fountains were placed (special hydraulic devices allowed the waters of the Acqua Vergine to be used).

In 1576 the villa was sold to Cardinal Ferdinando de' Medici, who lived there until 1587, when he became grand duke of Tuscany, as a consequence renouncing the cardinalate. He immediately summoned the greatest architect of the grand duchy, Bartolomeo Ammannati, to remodel the building according to a new design notable for its monumental facade on the garden side. The new facade—with a Serlian loggia and two *altane* (covered roof terraces) linked by a terrace—is derived from the model of the villa-museum. In order to create the remarkable decoration with ancient bas-reliefs, statues, busts, and architectural fragments, the cardinal purchased the famous collections of the Della Valle and the Del Bufalo. Other outstanding ancient sculptures were housed in the gallery-antiquarium wing next to the villa or were distributed around the garden.

Ammannati was responsible not only for the garden project but also for the terracing of the slope facing Rome. The garden formerly belonging to the Ricci, laid out in parterres and centering on an obelisk on the axis of the villa, was extended with the del Bosco terrace; the two gardens are linked by a long rectilinear approach that begins at the gate on Via Pinciana and ends on the opposite

VILLA MEDICI

side with the backdrop of the colossal statue of the goddess Roma (originally the imposing group of the Niobids was located here). Particularly interesting is the small hill of Parnassus created by covering over the ancient Temple of Fortune (on the axis of the exedra of the Lucullian Gardens) with a mound of earth crowned by cypresses modeled on the Mausoleum of Augustus.

The cascades and fountains flanking the flight of steps that led to the top of the belvedere mound no longer exist. A tower of the Aurelian wall was rebuilt as the Loggia of Cleopatra (it was then replaced by one dedicated to Venus), while another tower serving as the cardinal's pavilion and *studiolo* comprised a large room frescoed with a pergola (the frescoes, interesting examples of botanical and zoological art, have recently been rediscovered under the plaster and studied by Philippe Morel) and a smaller room with views of the villa, allegorical scenes, and grotesques.

From the late sixteenth to the end of the eighteenth centuries the villa was progressively stripped of its collections of ancient and modern works of art, many of which were sent to the museums and the Medici Gardens in Florence. The numerous cippi—mainly from Hadrian's Villa—and copies or casts of the originals now elsewhere are still present in the garden; they include the Niobids (in a compartment of the garden), the Dacians and the obelisk (in front of the villa), Mercury by Giambologna, and the lions (in the loggia of the villa). The rebirth of the villa dates from 1804, when it was taken over by Napoleon to house the Accademia di Francia, which was founded by Louis XIV in 1666 to allow young French artists to come to Rome to complete their training.

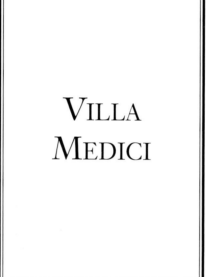

Left: The garden seen from Ammannati's Serlian loggia (from Percier and Fontaine, 1824).

Right: Detail of the ancient sarcophagus used as a basin for the fountain in the walled garden facing Trinità dei Monti.

Overleaf: Garden with the fountain and obelisk (copy of the original moved to the Boboli Gardens, Florence, in 1788).

DETAIL OF A DOLPHIN IN THE OBELISK FOUNTAIN.

IONIC CAPITAL OF THE SERLIAN LOGGIA OF THE VILLA (DESIGNED BY
BARTOLOMEO AMMANNATI).

Overleaf: Garden with
the obelisk and the retaining wall of the terrace
(designed by Bartolomeo
Ammannati).

Second overleaf: Ancient
sculptural fragments on
the retaining wall of the
terrace.

Third overleaf: Garden
with the obelisk and the
retaining wall of the terrace (designed by Bar-
tolomeo Ammannati).

D   N
C·VECILIAE
GALLITTAE
VIX·ANN·XXV
C·AECILIVS
PYLADES
SORORI·SVAE
PIISSIM·FECIT

DETAIL OF A VICTORY ON THE PEDESTAL.

LEFT: STATUE OF A DACIAN PRISONER IN THE GARDEN.

Overleaf: Details of the ancient *termini* placed in the garden to mark the beginnings of the paths.

MASCARON IN TRAVERTINE AND STUCCO ON THE PILLAR OF THE GATEWAY FORMING
THE ENTRANCE FROM THE PINCIAN HILL (REBUILT CA. 1770–80).

RIGHT: GODDESS ROMA (ANCIENT STATUE GIVEN BY GREGORY XIII TO
FERDINANDO DE' MEDICI).

Overleaf: Loggia of
Cleopatra. Built in 1576
on a tower of the Aurelian
walls, it now houses a
statue of Venus.

Second overleaf: Group
of Niobids in the garden
near the Pincian Hill
(nineteenth-century plas-
ter casts of the original
Greco-Roman sculptures
now in the Uffizi).

ABOVE AND LEFT: DETAILS OF THE GROUP OF NIOBIDS (NINETEENTH-CENTURY
PLASTER CASTS OF THE ORIGINAL GRECO-ROMAN SCULPTURES NOW IN THE UFFIZI).

ROOMS ABOVE THE WALLS. THE DECORATIVE CYCLE OF THE STANZINO DELL'AURORA (FRESCOES BY JACOPO ZUCCHI AND ASSISTANTS) COMPRISES THE WINDS, AURORA, ORION, THE SIGNS OF THE ZODIAC, THE SEASONS, AND SCENES FROM AESOP'S FABLES.

RIGHT: DETAIL OF THE DECORATION IN THE STANZA DEGLI UCCELLI (FRESCOES BY JACOPO ZUCCHI AND ASSISTANTS).

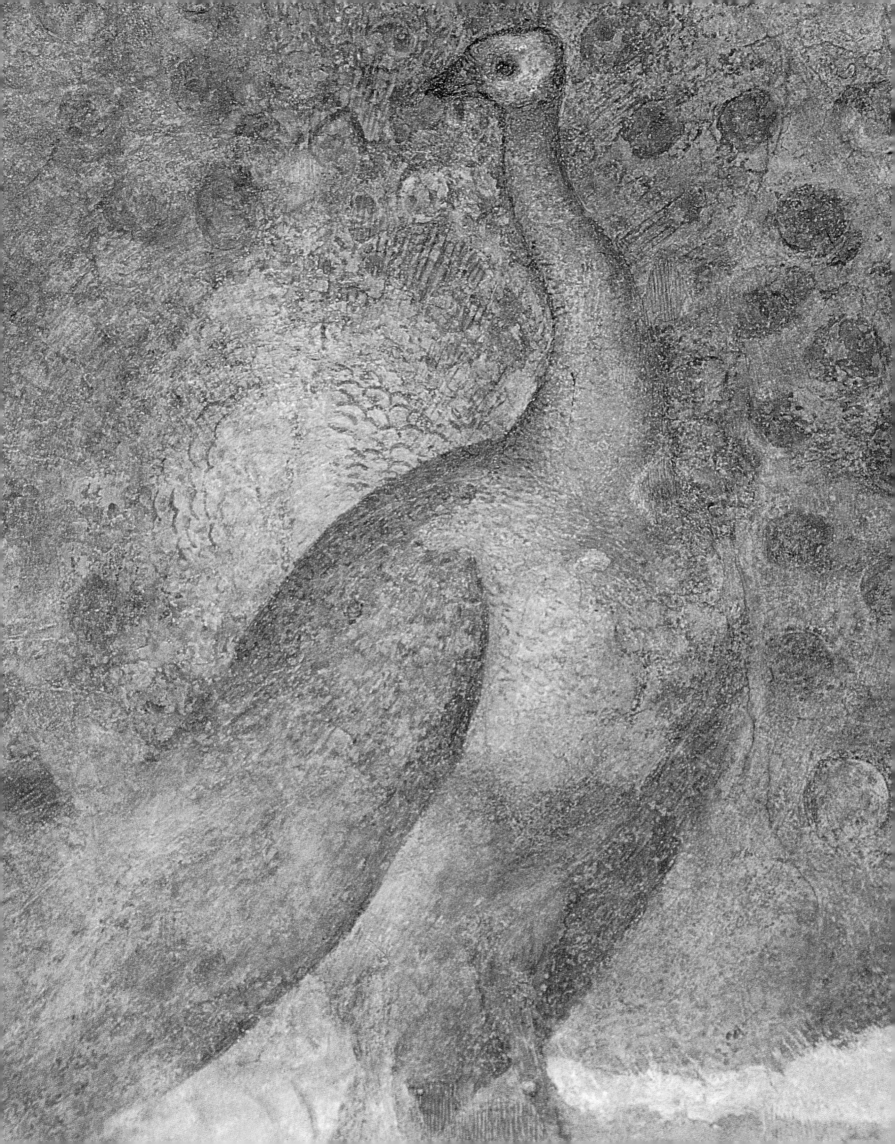

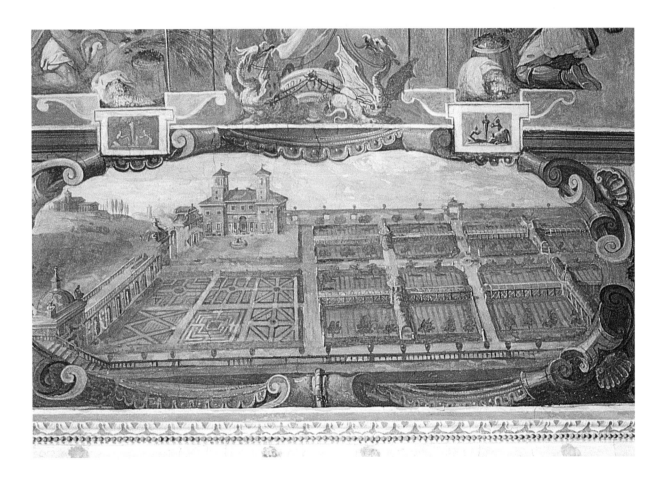

ABOVE AND LEFT: ROOMS ABOVE THE WALLS. THE DECORATION IN THE STANZINO
DELL'AURORA (FRESCOES BY JACOPO ZUCCHI AND ASSISTANTS) INCLUDES A VIEW
OF THE GARDEN REPRESENTING AMMANNATI'S SCHEME.

ONE OF THE TWO MEDICI LIONS ON THE TERRACE OF THE LOGGIA OF THE VILLA.

RIGHT: MERCURY FOUNTAIN (COPY OF THE BRONZE SCULPTURE BY GIAMBOLOGNA,
NOW IN THE MUSEO DEL BARGELLO, FLORENCE) ON THE TERRACE
OF THE LOGGIA OF THE VILLA.

Overleaf: Garden facade (designed by Bartolomeo Ammannati). An enormous surface for the display of antique reliefs from, above all, the Della Valle Collection, it was specially purchased for this purpose by Ferdinando de' Medici.

Between 1575 and 1577 Cecchino del Nero, a senior official in the Curia, of Florentine origin, built a casino on a Greek-cross plan in his vineyard on Via di Porta Pinciana (on the site of the ancient gardens of Sallust). In 1596 this was acquired by Cardinal Francesco Maria del Monte, an eclectic intellectual with erudite antiquarian, scientific, and alchemical interests, who commissioned Caravaggio to decorate the ceiling of the "small room of his distillery" with "Jupiter, Neptune, and Pluto . . . these gods taking possession of the elements with a globe of the world between them" (G. P. Bellori, 1672).

In 1621–22 the Nero–del Monte property, together with a number of adjacent vineyards, was acquired by Cardinal Ludovico Ludovisi (nephew of Gregory XV), who commissioned the leading Emilian painters of the day to decorate a number of rooms in the casino. These include the Sala dei Paesi (ceiling painting by Guercino with quadrature or architectural settings by Agostino Tassi; landscapes by Domenichino, Paul Bril, and Giovanni Battista Viola), the Sala della Fama (ceiling painting by Guercino with quadrature by Tassi), and the splendid ceiling fresco of the Aurora, Guercino's masterpiece, for which the casino was named. The cardinal then charged Carlo Maderno, the family architect, with the rebuilding of the Palazzo Grande, which formerly belonged to the Orsini.

VILLA LUDOVISI

The villa, which was located on the far side of a vast square adorned with a large Triton-shaped fountain (still extant), was entered over a three-arched bridge from which, by a double flight of steps, it was possible to descend to the *nymphaeum* below. The tripartite facade included a higher and more richly decorated central section linked to the side sections with large volutes bearing the Ludovisi heraldic bends. The rich, celebrated collection of sculptures—consisting mainly of ancient pieces (in 1622–23 Cardinal Ludovisi purchased the Cesi and Cesarini collections) and a number of contemporary works, including *The Rape of Proserpine* by Bernini—was displayed in the interior, in the park (with a *boschetto* or small wooded area in the form of a labyrinth of statues designed by Domenichino), and in a "casino with a gallery of statues." The park, soon renowned for its size and beauty, was laid out in a series of long tree-lined paths, leading to the backdrop of the Aurelian walls, forming the boundary wall.

In 1886, despite public concern, the property was sold by the Boncompagni Ludovisi as building land. The family kept only the Casino dell'Aurora and the Palazzo Grande; the latter was then incorporated into the sumptuous Palazzo Margherita, designed by Gaetano Koch and now housing the American embassy.

Left: Palazzo Grande (engraving by G. Vasi, 1761). The Casino del Nero, later dell'Aurora, is visible at the upper right.

Right: Ancient statue of a Roman consul.

VIEW OF THE GARDEN.

LEFT: DETAIL OF THE TRITON FOUNTAIN. EXECUTED IN 1633, THIS FOUNTAIN, FORMERLY ADORNED WITH GROUPS OF DOLPHINS AND PUTTI, STOOD IN THE CENTER OF THE SQUARE IN FRONT OF THE PALAZZO GRANDE.

DETAIL OF THE STATUE OF JUNO IN THE BOUNDARY WALL
(TOWARD VIA FRIULI).

RIGHT: DETAIL OF THE BACCHUS FOUNTAIN.

Overleaf: The large gallery (designed by Gaetano Koch).

DETAIL OF THE CEILING OF PALAZZO MARGHERITA.

RIGHT: DETAIL OF THE STUCCOES IN THE LARGE GALLERY (DESIGNED BY GAETANO
KOCH) OF PALAZZO MARGHERITA.

Above and left: Details of the stucco decoration of the ceiling in the large gallery of Palazzo Margherita.

Above and right: Details of the stuccoes in the large gallery (designed
by Gaetano Koch) in Palazzo Margherita.

CASINO DELL'AURORA. THE CEILING OF A ROOM ON THE UPPER FLOOR DEPICTS
JUPITER, NEPTUNE, AND PLUTO (WALL PAINTING IN OILS BY CARAVAGGIO).
THE ZODIACAL FASCIA CROSSING THE COSMOS REPRESENTS THE HOROSCOPE OF
CARDINAL DEL MONTE.

LEFT: ANCIENT BUST IN THE GARDEN.

Overleaf: Casino dell'Aurora. Lintels of the doors of the Sala dell'Aurora bear inscriptions of Cardinal Ludovisi's name.

L·CARDINALIS·LVDOVISIVS·CAMER

L·CARDINALIS·LVDOVISIVS·CAMER·

CEILING OF THE SALA DEI PAESI (FRESCOES BY GUERCINO, AGOSTINO TASSI, DOMENICHINO, PAUL BRIL, AND GIOVANNI BATTISTA VIOLA) IN THE CASINO DELL'AURORA.

LUNETTE IN THE SALA DELL'AURORA DEPICTING DAY
(FRESCO BY GUERCINO) IN THE CASINO DELL'AURORA.

DETAIL OF THE CEILING OF THE SALA DELLA FAMA WITH A FRESCO BY GUERCINO
IN THE CASINO DELL'AURORA.

CEILING OF THE SALA DELLA FAMA (FRESCOES BY GUERCINO, QUADRATURA ARCHITECTURE BY AGOSTINO TASSI) IN THE CASINO DELL'AURORA.

Overleaf: Ceiling of the Sala dell'Aurora (fresco by Guercino) in the Casino dell'Aurora.

In 1644, after Innocent X (originally Giovanni Battista Pamphili, pope 1644–55) had been elected pope, his cardinal nephew Camillo Pamphili began the extension of the Pamphili vineyard, beyond Porta San Pancrazio. Three years later he renounced the cardinal's hat to marry, despite his family's opposition, Olimpia Aldobrandini (a Borghese widow, and thus a member of the families possessing some of the most important villas in Rome and Frascati). The plans for the villa reflected the personality of the young patron, who was passionately fond of both literature and architecture. "Before his marriage, Camillo had identified himself with the family policy aimed at the attainment of universal power; then he proceeded to celebrate love as an individual gift and the origin of the universal equilibrium, concluding his inner journey with the exaltation of the arts, especially music and theater" (C. Benocci, 1996).

After rejecting designs by Borromini, Camillo Pamphili commissioned Alessandro Algardi, the family's sculptor and restorer, to design the villa. He was assisted by the Bolognese painter Giovanni Francesco Grimaldi. The original project envisaged two lower wings flanking the casino and terminating in pavilions; the facades were "real displays of ancient marbles," some of which had been excavated on the site of the villa itself and then heavily restored (I. Belli Barsali, 1970); other statues from the splendid Pamphili Collection were placed in the terraced gardens around the casino and inside the building in very refined stucco frames.

The gardens are among the largest in Rome (in the nineteenth century the prop-

VILLA DORIA PAMPHILI

erty covered 200 hectares, or about 500 acres). Their original layout, known through the remarkable collection of engravings entitled *Villa Pamphilia* (published by G. G. de Rossi ca. 1666–70), may also be attributed to Algardi and Grimaldi. Around the casino there were two walled gardens with numerous fountains (including that of Venus by Gian Battista Ferrabosco) and a Doric exedra or theater adorned with statues where plays and entertainments were held. This was reached from an area laid out in parterres in which the heraldic lilies of the Pamphili grew. The enchanting gardens were thus described on an engraving by Giovanni Battista Falda and Dominique Barrière: "myrtle hedges, a wood, flowers, statues, a theater; if this is not a feast to the eyes, then nothing else will be." The gardens were separated from the wooded area with a game reserve, the pasture, and the cultivated land by a strip of pinewood.

From the end of the eighteenth century onward the villa was extensively renewed. Francesco Bettini, who had trained in Paris and London, redesigned a number of areas of the garden in the Anglo-Chinese style for Prince Andrea IV Doria Pamphili. After suffering considerable damage during the siege by the French in 1849, and following the marriage of Andrea V to Mary Talbot, the whole park, with the exception of the formal gardens next to the casino, was laid out afresh in the English style. On this occasion Andrea Busiri Vici designed a number of additional buildings, including a new entrance to the villa with a porter's lodge, a chapel, and a monument to the French who fell in 1849.

O DEL PALAZZO CON DIVERSA VEDVTA DEL GIARDINO DEL BEL RESPIRO DELL EC^{mo} SIG PRENCIPE PAMPHILIO

Left: Casino del Belrespiro (engraving by G. B. Falda, 1676).

Right: Ancient bust on the facade.

Overleaf: South facade (designed by Alessandro Algardi).

FRAGMENTS OF ANCIENT SCULPTURES ON THE FACADE OF THE CASINO DEL BELRESPIRO.

FRAGMENTS OF ANCIENT SCULPTURES ON THE FACADE OF THE CASINO DEL BELRESPIRO.

Overleaf: South facade of the Casino del Belrespiro (designed by Alessandro Algardi). The fountain in the foreground is a nineteenth-century copy of the fountain by Pietro Tacca (1627) in Piazza dell'Annunziata, Florence.

ANCIENT SARCOPHAGUS DECORATED WITH A BATTLE SCENE, WITH THE PAMPHILI COAT OF ARMS
ABOVE (ANTONIO PIERUZZI, 1646), ON A FACADE OF THE CASINO DEL BELRESPIRO
(DESIGNED BY ALESSANDRO ALGARDI).

LEFT: RELIEF WITH FEMALE FIGURE (GIAN BATTISTA FERRABOSCO, 1646) ON A FACADE OF THE
CASINO DEL BELRESPIRO (DESIGNED BY ALESSANDRO ALGARDI).

ABOVE AND RIGHT: DETAILS OF THE FACADES OF THE CASINO DEL BELRESPIRO
(DESIGNED BY ALESSANDRO ALGARDI) WITH ANCIENT MARBLE BUSTS AND RELIEFS
REASSEMBLED OR RESTORED WITH STUCCO.

Detail of a sarcophagus decorated with garlands and theatrical masks
on the west facade of the Casino del Belrespiro.

Details of a sarcophagus decorated with garlands and theatrical masks on the west facade of the Casino del Belrespiro.

Overleaf: Side view of the Casino del Belrespiro (designed by Alessandro Algardi).

Above and left: Details of the decoration of the facades with busts, lion protomes, ancient marble bas-reliefs, and seventeenth-century stuccoes.

Overleaf: North facade of the Casino del Belrespiro (designed by Alessandro Algardi).

Detail of a trophy with a dolphin and lion on the Casino del Belrespiro.

Detail of a shield bearing a Medusa's head on the Casino del Belrespiro.

Roman statue of female figure.

DORIA PAMPHILI COAT OF ARMS.

In 1763, Cardinal Flavio Chigi (1711–71), "who did not have an opportunity to excel in the Curia and the political intrigues of his day" (P. Paschini, 1946), bought a vineyard with a casino at Monte delle Gioie on Via del Crocefisso. After he had enlarged the property by purchasing various adjacent plots of land, the cardinal transformed the casino into a villa, commissioning first the architect Tommaso Bianchi and then Pietro Camporese to add a new wing with an entrance hall, monumental staircase, chapel, and numerous new rooms. Until the cardinal's death, the work of decorating and furnishing the rooms and laying out the garden was documented in detail. Now largely lost, the garden was divided into two areas: one next to the villa, laid out formally in parterres with regular beds and box borders, citrus plants in pots, and clumps of holm-oaks and laurels; and a larger one with lawns, crossed by a long avenue of cypresses on the axis of the entrance hall. At the end of the avenue was a space with fountains and statues, closed by a balustrade, from which it was possible to descend by two symmetrically curved flights of steps to the path skirting the boundary wall (I. Belli Barsali, 1970).

In the rooms on the ground floor and on the piano nobile, paintings by Carlo Monaldi, Paolo Anesi, and Antonio Bicchierai (still partially extant) represent idyllic scenes of Arcadian life, "where, for the peasants, every day is a holiday" (A. Busiri Vici, 1975). These were clearly influenced by the literary current of which the Chigi were some of the leading exponents, especially the

VILLA CHIGI

•

SALA DELLA TEBAIDE

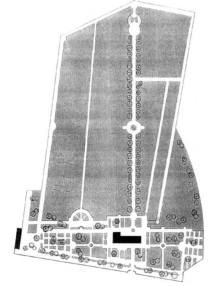

poet and Arcadian Prince Sigismondo (R. Lefevre, 1994). Particularly noticeable amid the pastoralism, dances, and genre scenes is the constant reference to the property of the family, especially their beloved estate at Ariccia.

The chapel and ante-chapel also belong to this remarkable theatrical complex: in the former, Bicchierai painted scenes from the life of the Virgin Mary "represented with the typical Arcadian character of a minor domestic chronicle" (A. Negro, 1996), while in the latter, around 1764, the otherwise unknown Francesco Nubale and Giacomo Rubini painted a Thebaïd in gouache. In contrast to the refined frames with Ionic colonnades of the previous rooms, the ante-chapel features a cavernous rustic shelter in ruins, with breached walls, broken beams, and staved-in doors, extending from the walls to the ceiling and doors. Through the openings, fragments of landscape are visible in which figures of hermits and friars of different orders are seated in meditation, prayer, or pious conversation. The genre of the "meditation room," hermitage, or Thebaïd (from the desert region of Thebes where, in the early centuries of Christianity, hermitism and monasticism flourished) was inspired both by a family tradition (the Chigi garden at the Quattro Fontane, now destroyed; the Villa Chigi at Cetinale) and the vogue current in mid-eighteenth century Rome, in the wake of the success of Charles-Louis Clérisseau's decoration of the cell of the fathers Jacquier and Le Seur at Trinità dei Monti (T. J. McCormick, 1990).

Left: Villa Chigi (plan from I. Belli Barsali, 1970).

Right: Detail of the ante-chapel or Sala della Tebaide (wall-painting in gouache by Francesco Nubale, ca. 1764) showing a friar in prayer.

Overleaf: Ante-chapel or Sala della Tebaide (wall-painting in gouache by Francesco Nubale, ca. 1764). The decoration covering the walls, ceiling, and doors simulates a ruined building.

ABOVE AND LEFT: ANTE-CHAPEL OR SALA DELLA TEBAIDE (WALL-PAINTING IN
GOUACHE BY FRANCESCO NUBALE, CA. 1764). THE DECORATION INCLUDES HERMITS
AND FRIARS MEDITATING, STUDYING, AND PRAYING.

ABOVE AND RIGHT: ANTE-CHAPEL OR SALA DELLA TEBAIDE (WALL-PAINTING IN
GOUACHE BY FRANCESCO NUBALE, CEILINGS BY GIACOMO RUBINI, CA. 1764).

The huge villa beyond the Porta Pinciana was built from 1608 on by Scipione Borghese, Paul V's powerful cardinal nephew. The area was subdivided into three enclosures having different characteristics: "The first enclosure, or 'woodland garden' was a sort of filter between the public and the prince. Accessible to all, on foot or in a carriage, its center was in the square in front of the palace, which also allowed guests to wait in the open. It was a shady area that could only be crossed along the avenues, since all the beds were protected with hedges around their borders; fountains, stone seats, and various ornaments, such as tall herms, adorned the place. The second enclosure, the 'garden of the perspectives,' or 'the prince's private garden,' contained an area thickly planted with shrubs next to a completely open field; the two walled gardens flanking the palace were the most refined thanks to the splendid displays of flowers and the richly decorated backdrops. The third enclosure, or park, comprised rural meadows where animals could graze and live, and a game reserve for the prince. Trees, shrubs, bushes, and grasses gave shelter and sustenance to fallow deer and gazelles, while the large pond in the bottom of the valley was the home of waterfowl" (B. di Gaddo, 1985).

The "casino nobile," designed by Flaminio Ponzio—after his death in 1613, the work was completed by Giovanni Vasanzio—was modeled on the palace-museum type. According to the sources, 144 bas-reliefs, 70 busts, 43 statues, and other ancient sculptures were inserted in the facade, in stucco panels and friezes (at the beginning of the nineteenth century the facades were stripped of many of their decorations and simplified by Luigi Canina). The palace—with a colonnade at the front and two tall towers and a loggia behind—still houses the outstanding collection of ancient

VILLA BORGHESE

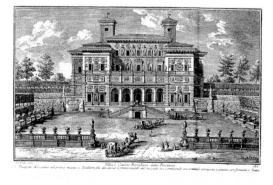

and modern works of art by Scipione Borghese; at the end of the eighteenth century the rooms were decorated with frescoes that were often attuned to the artworks displayed there.

It was proudly claimed that the villa was open to all, as an inscription attested: "Whosoever you may be, so long as you are a free man, fear not the hindrance of regulations; go wherever you will, ask whatever you wish; leave whenever you desire. These delights have been made for the visitor rather than for the owner. In this golden century, the owner refuses to impose strict rules on his guests. . . . If, however, with deliberate deceit, anyone should break the golden laws of courtesy, he should beware lest the angry keeper tear up the card of friendship."

Between 1776 and 1793 the western section of the villa was redesigned by Prince Marc' Antonio Borghese, who, together with the architects Antonio and Mario Asprucci, coordinated an international team of artists and decorators: W. Peter, Taddeo Kuntze, Cristoforo Unterberger, Giovanni Battista Marchetti, P. Rotati, Giovacchino Agricola, Giuseppe Cades, and Felice Giani. Particularly remarkable are the Tempietto of Faustina, a fake ruin, and the Giardino del Lago, with the Temple of Aesculapius in the center of a small artificial lake with sinuous banks inspired by the English landscaped garden.

With the completion of Luigi Canina's projects, commissioned by Prince Camillo Borghese, the villa was given its definitive layout and was extended toward the Porta del Popolo, with the creation of a new monumental entrance, the Greek propylaea, and a system of radial avenues converging on monumental backdrops in different styles, such as the Arch of Septimius Severus and the Egyptian propylaea.

Left: The facade of the casino of Villa Borghese with the original decoration (engraving by G. Vasi, 1761).

Right: Detail of one of the colossal ancient herms (restored by Pietro Bernini, with the assistance of his son Gianlorenzo).

Overleaf: Sala di Paolina (frescoes by Giovanni Battista Marchetti, ca. 1775–85) at Villa Borghese. In the center is *Pauline Borghese as Venus* (sculpture by Antonio Canova).

SALA DEGLI IMPERATORI, WITH *THE RAPE OF PROSERPINE*
(SCULPTURE BY GIANLORENZO BERNINI) IN THE CENTER.

SALA DEL DAVID, WITH *DAVID*
(SCULPTURE BY GIANLORENZO BERNINI) IN THE CENTER.

ENTRANCE HALL (DECORATED IN 1775–85 BY ANTONIO
ASPRUCCI AND ASSISTANTS).

LEFT: DETAIL OF ANCIENT STATUE OF A FEMALE FIGURE.

DETAIL OF A SARCOPHAGUS FRONT DEPICTING THE LABORS OF HERCULES.

RIGHT: DETAIL OF THE DECORATION OF THE SALA EGIZIA (FRESCOES BY TOMMASO CONCA AND GIOVANNI BATTISTA MARCHETTI, CA. 1775–85).

Overleaf: Ceiling of the Sala di David (frescoes by Giovacchino Agricola and Francesco Caccianiga, ca. 1775–85).

Detail of an ancient sculptural group in Room VI.

Left: Details of high reliefs with female figures and
a sarcophagus lid in Room VI.

SALA EGIZIA. THE PICTORIAL DECORATION IS INSPIRED BY EGYPTIAN MYTHS;
ORIGINALLY THE ROOM HOUSED EGYPTIAN SCULPTURES, WHICH WERE THEN
TAKEN TO THE LOUVRE.

RIGHT: GROUP OF AENEAS AND ANCHISES (SCULPTURE BY
GIANLORENZO BERNINI) IN ROOM VI.

THE BORGHESE HERALDIC DRAGON ON THE PALAZZINA DELLA MERIDIANA.

LEFT: DETAIL OF THE GATEWAY LEADING TO THE AVENUE OF THE SARCOPHAGI.

FOUNTAIN OF THE HIPPOCAMPI (DESIGNED BY CRISTOFORO UNTERBERGER;
SCULPTURES BY LUIGI SALIMENI, 1791).

CASINO DELL'OROLOGIO (DESIGNED BY NICOLA FAGIOLI, 1791).

DETAIL OF A LOTUS CAPITAL IN THE EGYPTIAN PROPYLAEA.

RIGHT: LION FOUNTAIN (DESIGNED BY LUIGI CANINA, 1824–28).

DETAIL OF THE LION ON THE CROWN IN THE FOUNTAIN OF THE ACQUA FELICE.

LEFT: TEMPLE OF AESCULAPIUS IN THE GIARDINO DEL LAGO (DESIGNED BY
ANTONIO AND MARIO ASPRUCCI, 1789).

Capitals of the pilasters and columns of the Tempietto of Faustina (designed by Mario Asprucci and Carlo Unterberger, it is composed of ancient architectural and decorative fragments).

Right: Detail of one of the two Borghese heraldic eagles on the top of the columns of the gateway forming the entrance to the Muro Torto (reassembled in the 1930s at the Porta Pinciana).